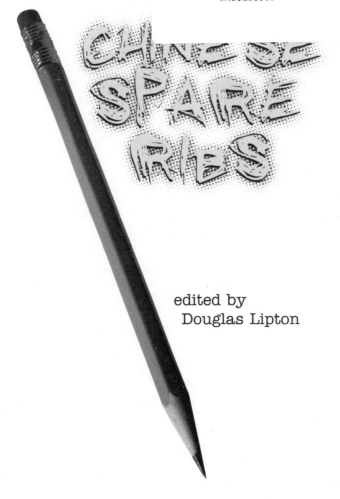

Chinese Spare Ribs

edited by
Douglas Lipton

Dumfries and Galloway
Libraries, Information and Archives
in association with
Dumfries and Galloway Arts Festival
1999

ACKNOWLEDGEMENTS

The editor and publisher would like to thank the following without whose involvement the YOUNG POETS competition - and, consequently, this anthology - would have been very different and less successful entities :

Dumfries and Galloway Arts Festival, particularly **Sheena Widdall** and **Jennifer Taylor**

James Thin's Bookshop, Dumfries - **Lorraine McLean** (Manager) and staff

David Gulland (Glass Engraver)

Vanessa Morris (Dumfries and Galloway Council's former Craft Development Officer)

Bernie Rutter (Sculptural Printmaker)

The Dumfries and Galloway Standard and **The Galloway News**

Markings

Radio West Sound and **BBC Radio Scotland (Dumfries)**

Scottish Power

Pupils and staff of the following local authority schools:

Borgue Primary School
Calside Primary School
Colvend Primary School
Dalbeattie High School
Douglas Ewart High School
Dumfries Academy
Dumfries High School
Dunscore Primary School
Eskdalemuir Primary School
Georgetown Primary School
Kelloholm Primary School
Kirkinner Primary School
Kirkcowan Primary School
Leswalt Primary School
Lockerbie Academy
Lockerbie Primary School
Maxwelltown High School
Moffat Academy
Moffat Primary School
Nethermill Primary School
Park Primary School
Rephad Primary School
St. Joseph's College
St. Ninian's Primary School
Sanquhar Academy
Troqueer Primary School
Wallacehall Academy

Pupils and staff at **Kilquhanity Private School**

Judges: Tessa Ransford, Dilys Rose, Stewart Conn, Valerie Gillies Donny O'Rourke.

Dumfries and Galloway Arts Association (with the **Scottish Arts Council**) - Writers-in-Residence Scheme.

First published 1999
© Poems remain copyright of their authors.
© Publication copyright Dumfries and Galloway Council

All rights reserved. No part of this work may be reproduced, stored in a retrieval system, or transmitted, in any form or by any means, electronic, mechanical, photocopying, recording or otherwise, without the written permission of Dumfries and Galloway Libraries, Information and Archives.

Designed, set and printed by Solway Offset Services, Catherinefield Industrial Estate, Dumfries for the publisher.

Dumfries and Galloway Libraries, Information and Archives,
Central Support Unit, Catherine Street, Dumfries DG1 1JB

ISBN 0 946280 35 5

INTRODUCTION

This book represents the enduring, diamond tip of a prodigious iceberg.

In 1994, the Dumfries and Galloway Arts Festival began, as part of its programme of literary and children's events, an annual poetry competition under the title YOUNG POETS.

Since its inception, the competition has attracted an average annual entry of 300 poems. Some entries are generated through publicity in local libraries, the local media and James Thin's bookshop in Dumfries (one of the event's sponsors). The greatest number of entries, however, comes from the region's schools. On the evidence of this competition, it seems that most young people in most of our schools, during most years, are regularly involved in the writing of poems - perhaps two or three a session. Clearly a great deal of time and imaginative effort is being expended in what our society may often seem to regard as an outmoded, irrelevant or, at best, minority form of literary expression.

If you are not an habitual reader of poetry, look at the writing in this book and decide for yourself whether poetry is outmoded or irrelevant. If you are a reader of poetry, this book will surely add to your conviction that poetry is alive and well as we enter the 21st Century.

Of course, as mentioned above, not all the poetry received by the competition comes from schools. It has become clear that much writing is being done by young poets at home as well - with or without encouragement - and it is also clear that little, if any, of its content matches the stereotype of adolescent self-centred, self-indulgent, soul searching - another of society's popular misconceptions. This 'independent' writing is committed, generous, sympathetic and lively.

From the beginning, the remarkable success of the poetry being produced by the YOUNG POETS of Dumfries and Galloway was evident. The idea was born for an anthology to contain some of the best work received by the competition in its first few years.

It is easy to be patronising and dismissive about the work of supposedly inexperienced writers. Occasionally, the collected works of a great poet will include a section of 'juvenilia' as an appendix. Perhaps, beside the mature work, this material will seldom seem to have more than passing academic interest. It is unfortunate that so much wonderful writing has a very limited audience - a teacher, some classmates, a sympathetic parent or friend. The work of young writers is seldom seen in print and is soon lost as time passes and priorities change.

Chinese Spare Ribs

Recognising that most of this huge volume writing, of which this book is a selection, is being done in schools, it must be assumed that it occurs as an assigned part of a course, a task or exercise to be completed as a curricular requirement. Although still successful as poetry, such writing may not usually appear to have a fulfilling life beyond the terms of the task in hand.

Moving away from its initial context, some pieces do begin to take on an independent life of their own, and a smaller number become perfect entities, pieces of true imaginative expression, fully achieved and realised. They are 'the tip of the iceberg' and it is a selection of these that is presented for the reader's appreciation in this anthology.

How true a reflection of all this poetic activity is the present volume? The sample that it represents has been put through a rigorous distillation : the young writers themselves make a decision about what pieces to submit; their choice is supported or influenced by their mentors; the judges of the competition make their assessments, with a tiny number of submissions getting the level of recognition that merits a prize or a commendation; finally, an editorial choice is also made.

The distillate here includes all prize-winners and commended poems since the competition's beginning. It also includes a substantial number that were perhaps temporarily stifled in their being 'overlooked' in not winning such a level of recognition. This collection hopes to let them breathe again alongside their publicly applauded fellows.

The poems contained in this anthology - while recognising quite clearly that they are written by people under the age of 18 - are of enduring appeal. They are vital, energetic, impassioned, funny, quirky, delightful, surprising, challenging, experimental, ambitious, sensitive, original - and very enjoyable. They all reveal a joy in language, a desire to find expression through the best use of words. These poems show their writers' caring about language.

Limited editorial control has been taken over the contents through the small task of adjusting minor irregularities of punctuation, spelling and presentation. There has been no other interference with the poems as presented - and all came with a mentor's guarantee of originality.

This collection of poetry will be exciting to any interested reader. It is bound to cause the hairs on the back of the neck to rise, to cause those shivers of recognition that we experience when we meet examples of creative perfection.

May 1999   **Douglas Lipton**

CONTENTS

SAM ALLISON
Chinese Spare Ribs 1

EMMA BAILLIE
Penguins 2
Scuil 2
A Tom Boy 3

ALANNA BARRON
The Lockerbie Air Disaster -
   21st December 1988
   or Fate Planned A Stop 4
Song of the Battery Hen 5

TESSA BARTLETT
Hello, Slimy, Slithery Snail 6

AUDREY BLAIR
The American Dream
   From Hope 7

MOLLY BRUCE
Outside 8

GEMMA BRYANT
My Mother 9

JAMIE BURGESS
Casualty 10

TALI BURGESS
A Pacifist In Wartime 11-13

MARY CARSON
Doctor's Waiting Room 14

KIRSTY CARSWELL
Rush Hour 15

MARIE CARTNER
Remembrance Day 11.11.18 16

MATTHEW CHANARIN
Harvest Moon 17

KELLY CLAPPERTON
3 a.m. 18

GEORGE CLARK
Hurcheon 19

HOLLY CLAY
Just Sitting : In Scotland 20
Michael 20-22

AIMEE COOK
Father To A Child 23-24

ANNIE COPLAND
The Bunnet-Laird 25

TASHA CROFTON
Fragments of Memories 26

DEREK CROOK
The Dead Eagle 27

ADAM CROSSAN
Wind 28

THOMAS DAGNON
The Chalk Board 29

SELENA DICKSON
Storm 30

MICHAEL DIGGINS
The Burning of Culmalie 31

Chinese Spare Ribs

v

STEVIE DOCHERTY
Rock Woman................................32

SARI EASTON
Bullying......................................33

KATIE FERGUSON
My Ex-Best Friend.....................34

CLAIRE FINLAY
Trainspotting..............................35

CATRIONA FITZSIMON
The Dolphin...............................36

JODI FRASER
Angel of the Sun........................37

ALLISON GARRETT
The Plant....................................38

WILMA GARRETT
Beachcomber...............................39

ROSIE GEORGESON
Tod...40

DARRYN GLEN
Florida..41

NICOLA GORDON
Childhood...................................42

DAVID GOVIER
The Innocent Face......................43
Two-Score Walkers In
   The Woods..............................44

ELKIE HAMID
Rubbish Dump...........................45

LORNA HAMILTON
The Lake.....................................46
Explosive Anger.........................47

LIAM HARKNESS
Water Is For...............................48

JAMES HENDERSON
Fairground Blues........................49

MARK HENDERSON
A Friend Is.................................50

KIRSTIN HOWATSON
The Price.....................................51

LORNA HOWE
Wetland......................................52

SHONTISHAR HYSLOP
Computerollergy.........................53

LAURA JACKSON
Morning......................................54

KARIN JAMIESON
Sea..55

LOUISE JOHNSTONE
Stalked..56

RODNEY KANE
Friday 13th of November............57

JOANNA LANE
The Puddock...............................58

KEVIN LENNON
Reflection....................................59

Chinese Spare Ribs

CHRIS LITHERLAND
Jason......................................60
Shadow..................................60
The Old Woman..................61

LORNA McAULEY
Death As A Stranger..............62
The Sailor.............................63

ALLISON McFARLANE
Afraid of the Dark.................64

ANNIE MacFARLANE
Scarecrow.............................65

EMMA McINTYRE
The Dentist From Hell...........66

KIRSTY McINTYRE
The Strange Bag....................67

LORNA McINTYRE
The Sea.................................68

DARREN MacLEAN
Number Castle......................69

LISA McLEAN
The Worries of a Sinner.........70

MARK E McLEOD
Back-biting...........................71

ANNE McMILLAN
The Leopard..........................72

KIRSTEN McMILLAN
My Dog Isla..........................73
The Snow Blizzard...........74-75

FIONA McTAGGART
The Bush...............................76

LUCY MACK
The Coast.............................77

LOIS MARSHALL
Spring...................................78

SCOTT MAXWELL
My Brain...............................79

STEWART MIDDLETON
Pharaoh................................80

LISA MILNE
A Little Too Perfect...............81

VALLA MOODIE
The Glass Eye.......................82

KIRSTY MUIR
Burns' Walk 19th
   January 1996.....................83
Summer Child.......................83
Symphony of War..................84

LAURA MUIR
My Sister's Hair................85-86

CHERYL MUIRHEAD
Your Invasion.......................87

KYLE MUIRHEAD
Birds Nest Anywhere.............88

NATASHA MURDOCH
She Hurts Ma Feelings............89

Chinese Spare Ribs

CLAIRE MURRAY
My Love Is Like A
Rainy Day........................90
To Stinking Socks.................91

ADAM NASH
Frog................................92

RICHARD NELSON
The Outcast.......................93

DENISE OBERN
My Special Friend.................94

DAVID OWEN
You!...............................95

BRET PARK
Homework...........................96

CARA PATERSON
Because It Was So Hot
That Summer.....................97
Bioloboob..........................98

CHRISTOPHER PHIN
Do You Take Drugs?
(*'normalised' version*)..........99

JULIE PIERCE
No More Elephants................100

LORELEY PLATT
Dragon............................101

ROSS PRESTON
Heroic............................102

ALAN PROVOST
The Fat Door Mouse...............103

ALAN RAE
Eyemouth Bay.....................104

HANNAH REEVE
Flower Arranging.................105
The Mushroom Ballad..............106
The Wizard Idea..................107

LINDSAY REID
The Door.........................108
Winter Haiku.....................108

CHARLOTTE RICHARDSON
Somebody.........................109

HAZEL RIGG
Dad'th Mouth.....................110

STUART ROAN
The Town By Night................111

REBECCA ROSS
Duick............................112
Swan.............................112

JEROME SCHERRER
Waiting..........................113

CRAIG SCOTT
Old Car..........................114

ROWENA ALEXA SEAGRAVE
The Big Parade...............115-116

SAPPHIRE SKILLEN
Hibernating......................117

NIGEL SMALLWOOD
My Old Farm......................118

viii

Chinese Spare Ribs

LEWIS SMITH
Which Witch Watched! 119

SAM SMITH
The Cool Blue 120

EMILY STEVENS
All Of Me 121
Mirror Image 121
Five Quiet Haiku 122

TRACY THOM
Sounds 123

AARON THOMSON
The Dead House 124

KAY THORBURN
I'd Rather Be! 125

LOUISE TROWBRIDGE
Myra Ratter 126

ASHLEY WALKER
The Sinking of the Titanic 127

SARAH WATSON
Lonely Cheap Glove 128
Megrin 128
Precious Bairn 129

ANGUS WEMYSS
Address Tae A Cra' 130
Peregrine 130
Swan 131
The White Harbour
(Port Ban) 131

PATRICK WEMYSS
Love 132
Sounds I Like 132
Tree People 133

NEIL C WESTGARTH
Beat the Devil 134
Revolution 135-136
Savages 137

STACY WILLIAMS
Reindeer Thief 138

IAN WRIGHT
The Attic 139
Sea 139
Hippo and Lion 140
Flower Murder 141

SHONAGH WRIGHT
The Intruder 142

Chinese Spare Ribs   *ix*

Chinese Spare Ribs

Chinese Spare Ribs

I like Chinese Spare Ribs.
They look like twigs but
They aren't oil rigs.
They taste like beef but
Some people say, "Good grief."
They have quite big bones and
They aren't ice cream cones.

Sam Allison

Penguins

are a crowd of old people
chatting away at a bus stop
then this cool teenager walks past
with his hands in his pockets
old folk still chatting
(no bus arrives)

a crowd of old people
chatting away at a bus stop
then this tramp slowly but surely
walks past
old folk still chatting
(no bus arrives)

Emma Baillie

Scuil

Scuil's a richt
if ye ken whoo te haunle the dominie.
Six fit twa he wis.
A haunled him in yin gan,
mouthin at me.
A jist stood up and said,
"Heh, big man, yer only a dominie;
no ma faither."
He sat doon in shame
and said sorry.

Emma Baillie

Chinese Spare Ribs

A Tom Boy

pretty froks frills an bows
fitba geer and a jeely nose

pink an white way ribbons fleein
makin ma mammy hit the ceelin

nails a cleen an curly hair
love getin dirty a the mair

plees, thankyou, excuse me, may ay
shift it buster or al poke your eye

Emma Baillie

Chinese Spare Ribs

The Lockerbie Air Disaster - 21st December 1988
Or, Fate Planned A Stop...

It was cold and dark in Lockerbie
When 103 took flight.
That 'plane soon turned to a fireball,
Exploding in the night.

The journey was from London.
America's where it would head,
But fate planned a stop over Lockerbie,
And, now, so many are dead.

They all died the week before Christmas
And many more lives fell apart,
All for the sake of vengeance
From someone with stone for a heart.

For a terrorist bomb was planted
On unlucky Flight 103,
But it burst in the sky over Lockerbie
Instead of over the sea.

The luggage was mostly presents
For children, or husbands, or wives.
But one of those parcels was deadly -
A gift taking hundreds of lives.

It wasn't just those on the 'plane killed,
For below, as we sat by the fire,
Together in terror we perished
In a furious kerosene fire.

All that remains is a garden,
To remember the many now dead.
I hope you will think of them always
As you lie, so safe, in your beds.

Alanna Barron

Chinese Spare Ribs

Song of the Battery Hen

I'm speaking today on behalf of us all,
That's Row 93, left-hand side, near the wall.
We want you to help us get out of this place
Where cruelty's a speciality and the food's a disgrace.

We're kept in cramped cages each long day and short night,
Not in the sun, but in fluorescent light.
I have no room to turn right around.
My eggs disappear through a hole in the ground.

My wings have been cut and my beak, it's been cropped.
My food tastes of feathers and chicken bits chopped.
But wait, the door's open. Come on, girls, let's go!
Hold on, what's this... A knife? No. No... NOOOO...

Alanna Barron

Chinese Spare Ribs

Hello Slimy, Slithery Snail

Where is your home, slimy, slithery snail?
    My home is my shell.
    It is part of my body.

Do you like the sun, slimy, slithery snail?
    No, I do not like the sun.
    It dries me up.

What do you eat, slimy, slithery snail?
    I eat flower leaves.
    I adore cabbages and lettuces.

How do you find your food, slimy, slithery snail?
    I find my food by smelling it out.
    I have a good sense of smell.

Who are your enemies, slimy, slithery snail?
    My enemies are birds.
    They crack me open and eat me.

What happens when danger lurks, slimy, slithery snail?
    I withdraw into my shell.
    I put a thin skin over the entrance.

Tell me about your horns, slimy, slithery snail.
    I have eyes at the end of them.
    I can't see very well with them, though.

How do you move, slimy, slithery snail?
    I use my muscular foot and slime gland too.
    It helps me move over rough surfaces.

Tessa Bartlett

Chinese Spare Ribs

The American Dream From Hope

"Though our challenges are fearsome, so are our strengths..."

Under the cover of night the evil spreads,
Stalking the seedy streets, ruthless, brutal, unharnessed.
The blood-splattered banner flies high over the violent streets
And Uncle Sam, along with the glory, is long dead and gone.
Sirens screaming warn of no return.
As the sun goes down, the fires burn.

"There is nothing wrong with America that cannot be cured by what is right with America..."

A cesspool of corrupt ambition - corporate greed is wealthy men.
Humanity is not big money.
The Big Apple is rotten to the core,
But the maggots thrive.
Neon lights sign the wild beasts' lair.
The American Dream is now a nightmare.

"Change to preserve America's ideals: life, liberty and the pursuit of happiness..."

The chewing-gum culture -
Sugar-sweet cheerleaders with dazzling smiles.
But Tinseltown is tarnished and doesn't shine,
And, behind the suits, the scandals are exposed -
The same culture, that sunny day,
Which blew away J.F.K.

"We must do what America does best : offer opportunity to all and demand responsibility from all..."

The homeless pave the sidewalk, cold and hungry,
But there's comfort in a bottle.
The city slums are filled with the desperate, the dangerous.
No hope, no light, no life.
The idealists' hope - the American Dream -
Breathed its last in a strangled scream.

Audrey Blair

Chinese Spare Ribs

Outside

Howling wind

Fog and snow

Rustling leaves

Blue sky

Rain and sun

And then a rainbow!

Molly Bruce

My Mother

My mother fell from the sky
From way up there - way up high
My mother is an angel without wings
So I try and give her flowers and those kind of things
My mother is good at art
She's very clever and very smart
My mother helps other ladies
Then she helps some children and she helps some
babies
My mother is an angel without wings.

Gemma Bryant

Casualty

Crash! We hit a car.
Ambulance was called.
Siren was heard.
Undertaker was ordered.
Accident was investigated.
Life was on the line.
Treatment was given.
Yellow flowers on the grave.

Jamie Burgess

A Pacifist In Wartime

Standing at the window, he watched
Like a child alone in the playground,
Wanting to join in, yet play different games,
But with courage enough just to wait
And hope that the chance would come later.
The soldiers marched by unaware,
Singing and saluting excitedly,
Like children going to the zoo for the first time,
And he felt like a parent
Who had to face the reality
Of animals in cramped cages.
He was like the zoo animals,
Stuck in a cage of his own making.
His brothers were among the soldiers,
Brave in a way he could never be.
But surely it was harder to fight with yourself
In a battle you could never win.

They would be coming soon
To take him with them
Or to another cage.
They wouldn't ask him anything
Or give him a chance to explain,
Silencing him like a criminal,
A fugitive without a voice.
Misrepresented, misunderstood,
They'd call him a coward
Or, possibly, even mad.
Yes, that's what they'd do :
Turn him into a madman
Who didn't know what he was saying.
He'd be pitied and 'understood'
By people he'd never known.

He could never tell anyone

Chinese Spare Ribs

That they were all wrong.
It wasn't just fear,
Although he felt that too,
So vividly he could almost touch it,
But sickness,
Sickness at the killing
And the false bravado,
Sickness at the young men,
Some little more than children,
Sentenced to die and be forgotten
In some far-off field without a name.
- All in the name of patriotism
He hated the very word,
Could taste it in his mouth -
The taste of blood and death and hopelessness,
The taste of what they wanted him to do :
To kill and maim and sing,
Sing songs of Britain proud
As he put men to eternal rest
With his 'faithful' machine,
Spewing out death
Like some deadly hose,
Before he joined them -
Another body on the battlefield.

That wasn't him -
Not a proud and victorious murderer.
He was a child,
A zoo animal,
A coward
Or a madman,
But not a murderer.
All he wanted was peace,
Peace and a chance to let them know
That death breeds death,
Not victory.
There are no winners,

Just losers;
Nothing to gain,
But everything to lose.

When the war was over,
In the future that seemed so far away,
People would look back and remember
Bombs, guns, conflict
And the brave soldiers
Who gave their lives
Or had them stolen.
But no one will remember
- For they are not worthy of remembrance -
The cowards and the madmen,
The pacifists in wartime.

Tali Burgess

Chinese Spare Ribs

Doctor's Waiting Room

I walk into the waiting room.
I sit down.
People staring, unseeing,
all in a world of their own,
deep in thoughts.
Telephones ring.
They pay no attention.
They're hoping and praying
all is well.

A young mother, baby crying,
her facial expression all of concern.
An old man coughs,
aged, weary and worn.
When more children enter,
his face lights up -
his thoughts of long ago.

White coat appears.
Young mother rises, baby now asleep.
An older woman looks up, sighs,
then goes on reading.
The door closes. All is quiet.
What fate awaits them?

Mary Carson

Rush Hour

Rushing and pushing,
Running along,
Fighting and fuming,
Along in the throng.
Aeroplanes drone,
Train horns blast loud,
Zooming through stations,
People all in a crowd.
Bikes flash past,
Choppers they whirr,
Alarms of cars,
People insured.
High heels tip-tapping
Fast down the street,
Then there's a riot
In the middle of the week.
Kids scream and yell.
What a pell-mell!
Tumbling and rumbling,
Clinking of change.
Eggs smash! People clash!
The sparks from the garage,
The people you meet.
Motorbikes whoosh
Just an inch from your feet.
Supermarket bags,
People yell from their jags,
A siren is heard,
Police, Ambulance in herds.
Will it ever be silent?
Will it never be empty?
Will it always be full,
Like lions and bulls?

Kirsty Carswell

Chinese Spare Ribs

Remembrance Day 11.11.18

Broken, shattered, rusty
Inside weeds, piece of cloth
Blood shed on the cloth
Helpless people dead
People pass by day by day
Graves broken
Just like an air raid shelter
Hear the faint scream from the graveyard
Why did it happen?
Help shattered.

Marie Cartner

Harvest Moon

Peeping over the crest of a hill,
A young child,
Eager and shining,
A growing sliver of what must be.
Shrouded in mist.
Effervescent.

Striding with
Majestic grace,
The full arc of the night.
A strong young man.
Perfection.

Hanging in space,
Waxing and
Waning
Before and
After.

A pock-marked grandfather
Gives way to the sun.
Miles away
And yet
So close.

Matthew Chanarin

Chinese Spare Ribs

3 a.m.

3 a.m.,
Morning,
She hangs high in the silver-blue sky,
Looking down on me as a mother on child,
Sympathetic, stern.
She strokes my face with her silver fingers,
Awakening something deep inside me,
Her pure white milk feeds a primeval earth.
She hangs high above giant forbidding mountains,
Dwarfing them in her superiority.
Insignificant, I realise her cold light controls the stillness,
Everything around me, a grey statue,
Reality becomes a figment of my imagination.
Then she is robbed of her beauty,
Silently caught unawares.
All is dark, her hypnotic grip is broken,
Released into a world of mundane chaos.
3.05 a.m.
Morning.

Kelly Clapperton

Chinese Spare Ribs

Hurcheon

A sma, sma hurcheon rinnin
Thru the girse su,
Suppin ma dug's denner
And flegging hin tae the girse.
His heid a oosie
And his hin is a stobbie.
The sma, sma hurcheon,
Gin hin tae ma hoose.

George Clark

Just Sitting In Scotland

Sitting
Just sitting
Sitting and watching
Sitting, with the rain
Pouring past my sitting
Stillness. It falls, and sitting
In the puddles, as I sit,
My head, with rain sitting
In beads on my sitting
Face. Droplets sit on my
Nose, which sits;
Sitting and watching,
Just sitting,
Sitting.

Holly Clay

Michael

I'd see red first - but I'd not hit him.
He's too sunny,
his smiles unfolding. He has three:
the first - he's agreeing, "You're fine;"
now he's sorry - mouth curled up in a grin;
but this one I know - he says, "I'm just happy."

He always pauses - then speaks.
I don't know his voice, but
I'd recognise the silence between,
filled by his empty smile
that says, "I'm just happy,"
and the feeling he creates
of being whole.

We always miss the collision course,
his mind, muddy
like puddles in the ground.

Tall and gangly He makes up words
he's not a giraffe from sounds
Schlups. Spling. Sploops.
"Es ist gut."

He doesn't call me anything.
His mother was German - the past is gone,
he - living for today, if he's here;
me - wondering what he sees
behind those cow eyes of his. He tells me:
confusion - in a smile - and pauses.
But he's not really mysterious.
Laugh. Laughing. Laughter.
I like the stories he tells
of cavorting cows, with jumping eyebrows
astride whirlpools of eyes
in which reality disappears, but detail floats.
Normal events with laughter, where a laugh
is involved and we always end
laughing,
but at the difference:
me at him,
him at the story

Dangling limbs - static, heralding
bobbly jumpers with curls
of inquisitive wool, stringy
but solid, like his stance as he enters the room,
his eye searching, alighting, he purposes forward,
a place chosen - a growth bending,
but under whose will?

Erect posture, scant frame encasing

Chinese Spare Ribs

a void of feeling - exposed in a hug
of close confidences which don't quite reach
his elongated fingers, raw in their nervousness,
continually working the pleated cushion,
ragged in its chewed tartan fitting.

A boy - almost a grandfather -
an immaculate dresser, in his way.
If a peach stone hits his shirt :
a crease. Thing is,
when he kicks my leg I wince behind
the smile, puzzling in my ordered mind
the self-control that isn't there
in his selflessness.

He could keep me warm, but -
he's lost his coat.

Holly Clay

Father To A Child

One drink too many, no fit night to drink anyway.
Flashing lights, paramedics, then, in the cold light
of day, a doctor with a set face explains the
technicalities:
"Didn't have much of a chance, I'm afraid.
Didn't feel any pain, sir. Went out like a light."

And then the child:
"Where's mummy? Can I see her, daddy?"
The hardest thing to say to a child?
I think so, yes.

"Remember Paws, the cat, sweetheart?
How mummy told you she was in Heaven?"
(She was always much better at this sort of thing.)
"Well, mum's gone to see her.
She's dead, you see, gone where we can't see her.
It's just me and you now, darling. I'll be mummy and daddy.

"You remember when your class did the Nativity play?
Your mother was so proud she cried.
Remember you were a little angel with wings?
Well, mummy's got wings now.
Yes, that's right, sparkly and shiny.
But, no, Mrs Barker didn't make them.
Mummy's in Heaven where she's always happy.
Yes, she can eat all the chocolate ice-cream she wants.
No! Don't ever say that! You don't want to be there!

"Oh, I'm so sorry, darling. I didn't mean to shout.
You see it's hard for me. I loved mummy very much.
Some day you'll see her again. Not for a very long time.
No, not in the holidays : a very, *very* long time away.
It's all right to cry. See, I'm crying too.
We'll say goodbye properly at the funeral, but she won't

Chinese Spare Ribs

be able to speak back.
Nana and Grandad will be there too. And you can draw a picture
for her grave.

"Yes, we'll all miss her, but she's around us. No you can't touch
her, but she's there.
I'll love you enough for the both of us, but she's still here watching
over you, loving you,
because you'll always be her little girl."

Aimee Cook

The Bunnet-Laird

Under the brig the bunnet-laird sits,
Courin fae the clatty rain.
Wi the buirdliest crummock cleikit in his haun,
He's chauvan tae bield fae the bowdirs.

He sits draiggilt tae the bone,
Bursled fae the bleffarts.
The puir man's fair forfochen
As he drees the driddlan weather.

Annie Copland

Chinese Spare Ribs

Fragments of Memories

I sat in front of the TV
And waved to the pterodactyl
Flapping across the screen.
I thought it was waving at me.

I knew what the surprise was :
A baby sister.
No one had told me.
But I knew.

It was *her* birthday,
Her presents, *her* cards.
But she was too slow
So I opened them myself.

A new house, a new garden,
Empty, echoing rooms.
Grass towering over me.
A jungle I wouldn't enter.

Meeting new neighbours,
Pink, floral cushions, carpet, sofa,
A colouring book to keep me quiet,
And a tall glass of milk.

A hedgehog in the garden,
A rush of excitement.
The baby carried out in her nappy,
But I missed it.

                              Tasha Crofton

The Dead Eagle

It lay there, motionless.

His eyes, once evil and sharp,

Now dull and blind.

His beak, once terrifying and hooked,

Now useless and still.

His wings, once strong and huge,

Now crooked and stiff.

His talons, once scary and powerful,

Now empty and bleeding.

His feathers, once shining and smooth,

Now broken and damp.

He would hunt no more.

The eagle was dead.

Derek Crook

Wind

The wind is trying to tell me something
By pulling and pushing me around,
A hushing noise, making me listen,
Humming in my ears, talking
In its strange way
That I don't understand.
My hood is blown off
To get my attention.
It flaps my trousers
And stops me from going
By blowing me back.
It hasn't finished yet.
Its story isn't finished,
The story
That I don't understand.
What is it saying?

Adam Crossan

The Chalk Board

If you look up close, you can see

the chalk dust floating in the air.

When you look carefully, you

can see the cracks on the chalk

board. You can even see the left-

over residue from yesterday's

dividing sums.

Thomas Dagnon

Storm

Swallow.
Ye o the blue sea
Swallow.
Lick not the surface
tempted.
But mind instead
be damned.
And forget ye not
the blue o the sea
as it
Swallows.

Selena C. Dickson

The Burning of Culmalie

based on a theme from a novel by Kathleen Fidler

Gentle sparks evolve to
Flames devouring the thatch
Grey smoke bellowing out of cracks
Puffing panting all through the house
Flowing through the roof
Flaring like fireworks with added
Gunpowder
Fires red as blood
Seeping through cuts and dying
The rain plunging down
Punishing the fire for killing
The house

Michael Diggins

Rock Woman

Yo. My mother was a hippy chick,
Taught me to be myself,
Raised me in the eco way
Not to stay upon the shelf.
My mother went to Greenham
With a bunch of happy kids.
They all ate out of lunchboxes
With daisies on the lids.
She wore long floaty dresses
And leather waistcoats too.
They had a lot of tassels
But they weren't from a zoo.
She marched upon the bases
Against the nuclear bombs.
They carried great big banners
And they sang some lovely songs.
She had a far-out girlfriend
With glasses, named Jocasta.
They mostly lived on soya beans
But sometimes they ate pasta.
She said they were the wonder years -
Brother, I believe her:
Once rockin' flower-power child -
She's now an R.E. teacher.

Stevie Docherty

Bullying

Cold, wet, confused, upset,
Sitting on the hill,
   in the dark,
      in the rain,
Looking at the clouds, feeling nothing but pain.

Lying to my family,
Everything's fine.
   Thinking.
I feel like dying.

Thoughts whizzing round, round.
      Faces.
      Waiting.
      Teasing.
      Hating.
      Jumbled emotions bottled inside.
        Anger.
          Crying.
            Death.
              Sighing.

I can't go on.
There is no use.
   My mind is screaming
   No more abuse.

Sari Easton

Chinese Spare Ribs

My Ex-Best Friend

My ex-best friend, foe or fiend,
Sometimes sad and sometimes stupid.
My ex-best friend, enemy or beast,
Stupid, silly, sad, sorry,
Sorry she fell out with me.
But before she was different,
Cheerful, contented, comfortable with
herself.
That was before she became vain,
Pompous, pontifical, pretentious.
But that was before

Katie Ferguson

Trainspotting

A penguin is a trainspotter, trying to find the right train
in the cold
snowy
mist of the old London railway station.
He is trying to find the right train
but the mist
swirls round him. It almost
blinds the
poor
shabby
old penguin.
The penguin cannot find the right train.
Just three minutes late,
he mutters.
He starts to trudge back to
his home.
Some home.
The penguin you see is a tramp,
so his home is
plastic bags
cardboard
an old umbrella
a torn blanket
and a battered collection of old clothes
which has in it
a bow-tie
hat
and coat
which he somehow never seemed to throw away.

                                        Claire Finlay

Chinese Spare Ribs

The Dolphin

The dolphin dives and dines down in the deep.
He swims with a sparkle of splendour as he slices through the sea.

His body looks big and blue as he bounds beside the boats.
His fins and face look fair and fine.

He lingers, looking among lead crags, lunging at lobsters.
But one great fear got stuck in his grey matter - the gigantic jaws
of the great white shark.

Catriona Fitzsimon

Angel of the Sun

She caught the sun in her hair
and invited it to stay.
Her eyes are indistinguishable -
green, purple, maybe blue.
Clothes flow. They form her body.
Fairytale white, as minds suggest.
Her steps float off the ground.
No-one looks down past her.
No-one sees air flowing under.
Circles of pure colour and light.
Stars in her eyes tease smiles from others.
An angel she may be,
but the question isn't there.

Smiling to everyone, smiling at everything,
she wanders down the hall.
"Angel, angel, smiling sweetly,
with your touch will you greet me?"

Air meets closed eyes under clear skies.
It cools her thoughts. Lips part in thanks.
Smiling, smiling, dancing down streets,
angel brings happiness to those she meets.
Her breath gives warmth, her voice comfort.
Innocence is her light, shy eyes.

High, light, her bright mood
meets the boy behind the counter.
Smiling, smiling back, she reaches into her bag.
Blackness, sheen, changes her image.
Her hair seems duller. Her sweet more sickly.
But the smile remains.
And,
as the gun rips through him,
the floor disappears.
She dances down the street,
smiling, smiling.
An angel of the sun.

Jodi Fraser

The Plant

I remember the day I bought that plant,
I was in Dumfries with my Uncle and Aunt.
As soon as I saw it on the market stall,
I had to buy, if I had any sense at all.
I was drawn towards it in an alarming way.
If I didn't make it mine, I knew I would pay.
I put it in the kitchen as soon as I got home.
I looked after it and fed it as it was my own.
It grew very tall at a terrible rate
And, soon, whatever was near became what it ate:
The table, the cooker and, even, the door,
And, as it grew bigger, it ate even more:
The fridge, the freezer, my poor Uncle and Aunt,
Who were with me the day I bought that plant.
In the end we had to do something,
Otherwise we'd be left with nothing.
We hired a hit-man to put it to an end,
But it snapped so much he went round the bend.
Eventually it was my Nan
Who came up with a foolproof plan.
She whacked with her small handbag
And its leaves began to sag.
She carried on, but it could take no more.
It just collapsed onto the floor.
So that was the end of my beloved plant
That I'd bought at Dumfries with my Uncle and Aunt.

Allison Garrett

Beachcomber

Monday I found a sock,
sandy and soggy.
It's like one of my dad's.

Tuesday I found an earring,
wet and rusty.
It's like my mum's she wore to her
wedding.

Wednesday I found a hat
full of sand.
I marked it where the tide came in.

Thursday I found nothing
- just a man
selling hot-dogs and burgers.

Friday I found a chain,
a dog chain.
It said : Please return to ___ if found.

Saturday I found a ten-pound note.
It was wet and soggy.
Then the wind came and blew it away.

Sunday I found a watch.
It didn't work.
It was gold without a strap.

Wilma Garrett

Chinese Spare Ribs

Tod

The tod seelently danders
Along the garden, throu gate,
Wi heez lang reid runt sloggern behin him.
He sniffs the air saftly.
Tod, tod, tod.
Ma neb an ma een are verra sair
Kis I had a mishanter
When I ran intae a hoggie.

Rosie Georgeson

Florida

Splashing killer whales,
splashing, splashing,
to make you go breathless.

Scorching sun,
scorching, scorching,
like you are sitting in a fire.

Mickey Mouse laughing,
laughing, laughing,
to make you laugh too.

Winnie-the-Pooh eating,
eating, eating honey too,
honey, honey,
to make you eat too.

Lovely hotels,
lovely, lovely,
a swimming pool to swim in
and a restaurant to eat in.

But, oh! - What a shock it will be
to go home and let Florida be.

Darryn Glen

Childhood

Childhood was laughter,
Childhood was games.
Childhood is forgotten,
Life is not the same.

Childhood was fun,
Childhood was toys,
Childhood was friends,
Girls as well as boys.

Childhood was primary school,
Childhood was five times table,
Childhood was "The Singing Kettle".
It was built around a fable.

Childhood was innocence,
Childhood was cute.
Childhood was dressing up
In your Mother's best suit.

Childhood was parties,
Childhood was frocks,
Childhood was ribbons and bows
Tying up those golden locks.

Childhood was smiling faces,
Childhood was tears - well, only some.
Childhood was unsuspecting,
We didn't know what was to come.

Your childhood doesn't last.
Enjoy it while you can.
Your memories and you will stay together,
You can remember them forever.

Nicola Gordon

Chinese Spare Ribs

The Innocent Face

The teacher slams the door shut.
Subdued scribbling sets the sullen scene.
A whisper.
The teacher's eyes pounce like a tiger.
Silence.

An innocent face drops.
He is the hunter's prey.
Elsewhere, chairs scrape against the grey floor,
the same cold, unforgiving floor
which he now stares at,
in front of the biggest desk, which is the teacher's.

His hands seem confused -
they don't know what to do.
They start to tremble and shake.
Suddenly!
From the back of the class
comes a suppressed giggle.
More terrifying silence.
"Come here, boy...now!"
The innocent face should now be safe.

David Govier

Chinese Spare Ribs

Two-Score Walkers in the Woods

Glinting among earth was the rounded cheek of a Johnny Walker bottle,
Corked and soil-weathered for five decades five inches underground,
It left a smoothed trough long formed around it. But, better, promised
more.

Breaking the pucker-holed, polished indent with scrabbling dirty hands,
Swiping away the weather-worked dark heavy clay revealed more glass.
At first just a cool hard reflex jolt to a fingertip; an expected surprise.

Then, caressing along its curve, a clear trail across the shoulder was
Unearthed, leading to the choked cork neck. Yanked out, with a dry
splurge,
Into bright wooded sunshine, it shone and lit the nimble amber corner.

Thirty-seven more hidden swigs, most half-bottles, lay lined like glass
dolls
On the firm surface, transformed from empty dark furtive coffins into
living antiques,
Their hips shining like rows of sparkling eyes, wondering at the light
bright air.

Resonant clinking as the box was filled gave voice to line of can-can
ghosts,
Singing, flicking their skirts, flashing intoxicating smiles for the last time
and the
First time in a lifetime. Fleetingly savoured, laid down empty, and
forgotten again.

David Govier

Rubbish Dump

rusted cans crumble

moulded turnip ends

minutest scraps

banana skins

malleable as mud

turned-over chairs

decaying legs

piled high and

house shaped

one doll on top

with a flourished

ruptured head

Elkie Hamid

The Lake

An explosion of life
as each creature
works in time.
Every creature with its own path
and its own way to follow its path.

A kingfisher hovers over
the peaceful lake,
a predator
waiting for its prey to step out of line,
waiting,
watching,
and suddenly it's away diving
                    in
                         and
                                out
a minnow in its bill
snatched and gone.

Lorna Hamilton

Explosive Anger

As I watched I scented
destruction,
as the ferocious bolts of lightning
tore through the clouds
in a rage of anger,
as it surged through
the night sky
seeking revenge for its
imprisonment in the tightly
knotted clouds.
As it broke away the
anger raged inside the clouds,
when suddenly
the clouds were pushed apart
as the rest of the angry prisoners broke out
and tore through the sky
at blistering speed.
The clouds crashed back together
as the prisoners broke away.

Lorna Hamilton

Chinese Spare Ribs

Water Is For...

washing up the shore,
churning up rock,
making sand,

rushing down the street,
flowing along pipes,
dropping down drains,

wetting my sister (third change of clothes),
scooshing her on the head,
squirting her all over,

freezing the greenhouse,
raining down hard,
dripping.

Liam Harkness

Fairground Blues

Children eating hamburgers greedily

Little boys pestering their dads for another 50p

Clapped-out clockwork carousels getting stuck

Bits of squashed chewing-gum littering the ground

Lazy ticket-sellers persuading you to have one more go

Demented goldfish swimming round and round in a tiny poly bag

Pop music blaring out, blotting out all other noise

Gaudy lights with flickering bulbs on the point of failure

Fat women selling popcorn and candyfloss in a cheap old caravan

Bored wives crying out to their equally bored husbands

"I hate this place"

James Henderson

Chinese Spare Ribs

A Friend Is...

Someone you can rely on,
Someone who is kind,
Someone who's a good sidekick,
Someone who protects me,
Someone who makes you feel better,
Someone who's a good companion,
Someone who listens to you,
Someone that you care for,
Someone you can play with,
Someone you can go to town with,
Someone who will help you,
Someone who plays computer games with you,
Someone who gives you presents,
Someone who will respect your thoughts,
Someone who will give you peace,
Someone to share secrets,
Someone who trusts you and you can trust,
Someone who stays the night at your house,
Someone who makes you feel safe,
Someone who makes you happy,
Someone who is always there for you,
Someone who has the same feelings all the time,
Someone who does not hurt you,
Someone who sits beside you,
Someone who is friendly to you,
Someone who gives you a lot of good company,
Someone who isn't selfish to you,
Someone who isn't bad and nasty to you,
Someone who doesn't bribe you,
Someone who never fights or threatens you,
Someone who is joyful and merry,
Someone who will like you,
Someone who shows you respect.

A friend is a friend.

That's what a friend is!

Mark Henderson

Chinese Spare Ribs

The Price

Under the motorway I sit
Ten other kids just as me
Round a burning fire
Cardboard boxes as our home
No parents to go to

No food to eat
My stomach cries out
Empty as a desert
A dried up river with no fish
Brought to the slaughter

Under the motorway I sit
The kids' home
No adults allowed
Not since that day
The adult said there is a price we have to pay

The adult came and took my coat
A knife in one hand
Me in the other
Blood so red down my face
It stained me like a dying grace

He took our lives as an eagle with its prey
So innocent we used to live
But now we have the key
The key to another world
Another place

Never did the adult come again
But fear is like breathing barbed wire
Some never sleep
In fear of never waking again
In case the adult comes again

Kirstin Howatson

Chinese Spare Ribs

Wetland

The sun is setting over the flat wetlands reflecting on
Muddy shallows,
Making a carpet across the ground,
The smudging sun faintly fading over the horizon,
Dark trees reaching to the sky faintly disappearing as
It gets dark.

Fishing nets reach into the distance like giant
Spiders' webs,
Like a huge patchwork quilt.

I can hear geese squawking, quacking, flapping, honking hungrily
After their long journey,
Wind whistling through a solitary tree,
A barking dog,
Lapping water.

I can smell a salty smell,
Slimy seaweed wrapped around stones like presents,
Making blankets of seaweed over the stones,
Winkles and barnacles clinging to rocks like white pearls,
Rock pools where sea anemones hide.

I like standing watching the geese.
Winter is coming. It's getting cold.
It's lonely, quiet.
The rain is pouring down.
I decide to go home to a warm fire.

Lorna Howe

Computerollergy

Silver disc runs in the tower.
A button click.
A picture flick.
This machine's got power.

Cat sat on the mat. Or
Was it just a mouse?
With wires and buttons in every room
This computer's taking over the house.

Upgrade, download,
Copy this and run.
Save it, print it, clear it.
This doesn't sound like fun.

Fed up. I cannot type.
What is all this computer hype?
I do so little, achieve so much
With only just a clumsy touch.

O clever computer - what facility!
Unlimited RAM, endless capacity.
But nothing works - and here's the con -
Until *my* fingers turn it on.

Shontishar Hyslop

Chinese Spare Ribs

Morning

I see again the Fabergé gold of his hair
like the tendrils of this dream half-remembered
that wind web-like round my heart
as his arms embraced my spirit's shell.

Together we walked nowhere for miles and miles.
Cloaked in moonlight melded with love's
archaic radiance we were safe,
shielded from contemporary darkness
that lingered, vulpine.

Too soon morning's inverted alchemy turned gold to lead.
Alone beneath the sullen skies of an alien world
I clutched at the shadow of his name like a talisman
and longed for a fleeting eternity in his arms.

But the cloned changeling lights
have devoured the shadow and I am truly alone
with the millennium's pyrites promises
and the amaranthine darkness.

Laura Jackson

Sea

Back and forward,
Back and forward
Is what the sea does all day long,
The fish under it,
The children swimming in it.
What do all the creatures do?
Swim eat swim eat.
Or do they have an adventure?
Do they wake up,
Have breakfast,
Go and annoy the shark,
Get chased by a whale,
Go and have lunch with their family,
Meet up with their mates,
Go and speak to the mermaids,
Go home and have tea
And go to bed?
Or do they just
Swim eat swim eat,
Back and forward,
Back and forward,
All day?

Karin Jamieson

Stalked

My only light is a pale ribbon,
Slanting onto the road.
The silence is thick and choking,
Claustrophobic
And threatening,
For it is brief.

Determined footsteps jar the silence,
The footsteps
Of a crazy person,
Tormenting and cruel.
They mean he is coming nearer
And that means death.

And now you know
That I am stalked by a madman,
That every step I take
He is following,
That he craves death -
Mine - sure to come soon...

And suddenly the footsteps quicken,
Faster, faster,
Until they are running,
Bringing death with them,
For, when I turn, I see only a knife
And my whole existence as it passes before my eyes...

Is this Heaven
Where I am now?
The floating sensation?
The blackness?
It must be, for being stalked
Was a living Hell...

Louise Johnstone

Chinese Spare Ribs

Friday 13th of November

On Friday the thirteenth of November
Something happened which I remember:
I was walking home in the blistering rain
From the town of Coleraine.

Suddenly I heard a terrible bang,
And that there sound just rang and rang;
I looked around and saw a flame
In the town of Coleraine.

So I ran back towards the Town Hall,
Watching all the buildings fall;
Then I saw the people's pain
In the town of Coleraine.

There were looters running round at places,
While people watched and covered their faces.
I started walking home again
From the town of Coleraine.

I knew it was the I.R.A.
Who caused Coleraine's unlucky day.
Really, I think that they're insane,
Bombing the town of Coleraine.

Rodney Kane

Chinese Spare Ribs

The Puddock

His heid so still,
His een so staring,
Just sitting doon,
He disna rin,
Jist hunkers there.
A bug flees past.
GOBBLE!
Gin awa, Mr Flea.

Joanna Lane

Reflection

I remember a man who
Had stood before a congregation:
He was grey-haired and he wore a
Green tegument with grapes and
Yeast signifying Bread
And Wine. He had stood for years
Before these people and he had talked
About the life of a man:
The life of a real man; not a man who
Would impress a Bishop or another
Clergyman; not a photograph.

When the man, before his church,
Told them he wished to be a father,
They shunned him; called him a
Corruption; replied to him: bastard.
And yet.
 When they began to listen
To the sounds of the stream that
Wound its way around their town;
Among the trees, the birds;
The horse that would gallop
And steam on Summer days;
When the snow fell in gliding clumps:
Graceful and clumsy,
 The people understood how real
A man Jesus had been, and when the
Priest's wife conceived they
Smiled quietly, reflecting on
The stubbornness that they had
Believed was religion.

Kevin Lennon

Chinese Spare Ribs

Jason

A dark and lonely glade of trees
and mighty Jason, tall and fair.
Upon a hill so dark and grim
stood Lord Jason, straight and tall,
and in the glade a light was seen
from many a mile afar, away.
And there he heard a choir sing
so sweet and gentle, far away.
Yet in the night a shadow crept,
a darkening cloud toward the moon,
and far away the break of day
crept stealthily toward the sky,
a silver stream by Jason's feet,
it leaped, it jumped so bright and gay.
A silhouette of Jason now,
as daybreak fell into a cloud.
Oh, praise him, lord so strong so brave!
The church bells ring o'er Jason's grave.

Chris Litherland

Shadow

Upon this lake
I've always been
and on the shore
the flowers of spring
arise and fall like night and day.
But though I'm nigh I never touch
the golden dust
upon the land,
the golden dust
around the lake.

Chris Litherland

The Old Woman

Down the deep, everlasting alleyways,
Footsteps patter upon rotting stone floors,
And now down alleyways that once were fields,
Fields that once bore flowers,
Alleyways of memories, behind her now and
Unredeemable,
No dawn, nor any sweeping dusk may change these alleyways,
Alleyways of memories,
Alleyways of past time.

Chris Litherland

Chinese Spare Ribs

Death As A Stranger

Hello? Who's there?
Who knocks on my door at this dead hour?
The cock has yet to sound its call
And the last is long past gone,
Yet still,
You knock.

Hello? Who's there?
Who enters my house in the dead of night?
The sun has yet to rise the morn
And the last is long past gone,
Yet still,
You enter.

Hello? Who's there?
Who calls my name from those dead tones?
The morn has yet to call the day
And the last is long past gone,
Yet still,
You call.

Hello? Who's there?
Who touches my hand with that dead shiver?
The wind has yet to breathe its sigh
And the last is long past gone,
Yet still,
You touch.

Hello? Is it you?
Who enters my house at this - dead - hour?
Has the cock called soon
For the light is entering my window
And the wind is touching my neck.
Yes, I'll take your hand.
I enter.

Lorna McAuley

The Sailor

I stood still. Cold. He lay before me, dead, upon the
shattered glass of the sitting-room table. Life carved
its way across his forehead and joined the tide of blood
which was slowly surrounding him. The fog call from the
harbour mouth flooded with a rush of emotion as, anchored
by the weight of his achievements, I watched him drown
amid his thirsty temper.

It was dark. Silent. Drunkenly, I stood clutching the
bullet-powered steamship which had set him sail for the
final time. Death lined the stern twists of my face and
was carried slowly beyond the unchartered wynds of my
turbulent mind. And, with the buoyancy of lost men, we
lay, spread-eagled on the floor of a stained-glass raft,
drifting out on a sea of burgundy.

Lorna McAuley

Chinese Spare Ribs

Afraid Of The Dark

I think of you now, innocent but parasitic,
Your hand reaching to mine, but never getting there.
You were afraid of the dark, then.
I remember nursing you in my arms.
My blood ran cold as I watched you.
You were not wanted.

I try to block from my memory your cries,
Ones which you knew I would never comfort.
I could barely touch you, did you know?
You grew tired of me, your arms no longer
Gripping me.
Your cries were ignored. I cried then,
The sound echoing through the empty corridors
Of our house.

There is no possible way to reach you now
You are gone,
Sent away in an ebony-coloured box.
I, your mother, too cowardly to look at you,
Lying in your box,
No longer crying,
No longer clinging to my arms,
And no longer afraid of the dark.

Allison McFarlane

Scarecrow

Scarecrow,
Why do you watch,
Stare through the valley
And beyond and beyond?

Scarecrow,
Were you always so old,
So powerless to the wind
As you gaze, as you gaze?

Scarecrow,
Was there a time long ago?
Is that why you look
So deep, so deep?

Scarecrow,
Must you stand motionless
Through snow, through rain?
Do you cry, do you cry?

Scarecrow,
So alone,
You are proud, yet humble.
Can that be, can that be?

Annie M. MacFarlane

The Dentist From Hell

Drill in one hand, syringe in the other.
Screaming won't help, so I wouldn't bother.
Spotless gloves, white as his victim's teeth.
Angelic smile, but Satan underneath.

Children fear him; even the adults do.
Who's his next victim - could it be you?
His bloodstained overall, no longer green.
Taking people's teeth out - he seems awful keen.

His little mirror and chair of doom.
The smell of fear when you walk in the room.
The dreaded drill, his deadly weapon.
Children hate it; you hear them yelping.

So brush your teeth every day and night,
Or be prepared for a toothless fright.
Make sure your teeth and gums are well,
Or be ready for an appointment with the dentist from hell.

Emma McIntyre

The Strange Bag

There was an old man
walking glumly along the streets,
his staring eyes following you
wherever you go,
his broad narrow hat
like an eagle's beak.
There was a bag,
a strange bag.
It was an old bag.
I blinked
to see if I was dreaming.
He was GONE.
Only the bag remained,
lying there.

Kirsty McIntyre

The Sea

There was a sea
and on that sea
there was a boat
and on that boat
there was a man
and not a move
made he.

And with that man
there was a girl
whose hair was as
still and calm as
the sky
and not a move
made she.

But with that girl
there was a child
who was wrapped
up in a shawl
her lips as blue
and bluer than
the sea
and not a move
made she.

I walked along
the shore that
day and saw that
boat upon the sea
as still as space
and as cold as stone
and in it lay her
passengers three
and not a move
they made.

Lorna McIntyre

Number Castle

Ten knights at the Round Table.

Nine guards in bed.

Eight cooks cooking for the King.

Seven bags of gold for the King.

Six prisoners in the dungeon.

Five jugglers juggling for the King.

Four stuffed chickens for the King to eat.

Three horses getting a drink.

Two blacksmiths making horses' hooves.

One King in his castle.

Darren Maclean

The Worries Of A Sinner

Is forgiveness unconditional
If the person feels regret
Must it be a thought or word
An action or a threat

Because if forgiveness is unconditional
What becomes of sin
Does it count if it is a mere mistake
Or must evil come from the heart within

And if forgiveness is unconditional
Then what becomes of hell
Because if mistakes in life are not allowed
That is the place where I'm to dwell.

Lisa McLean

Back-Biting

My sister is a snake...
She goes behind my back.
She coils herself around my legs
And gives me lots of flak.
A hole for her I'd like to make,
But really she's not so bad a snake!

My sister's a snake in sheep's clothing:
She always pretends to be good,
But when there is no one looking,
She hisses and starts being rude.
A hole for her I'd like to make,
But really she's not so bad a snake!

A snake is slippery, sneaky and scary
And moves along on its belly:
I'm glad my sister's not so big
As the ones I've seen on the telly!
A hole for her I'd like to make,
But really she's not so bad a snake!

I suppose I'll have to put up with her
In spite of her sizzling moods,
But I'll always be wary of the snake in her,
Especially when she's good!
A hole for her I'd like to make,
But really she's not so bad a snake!

Mark E. Mcleod

Chinese Spare Ribs

The Leopard

In the silent black forest a rustle of the breeze is heard.
A beautiful animal rises from the shadows.
The sleek spotted coat jumps so quickly and disappears behind a tree.
Two gleaming torch-lights come from the forest,
its eyes glinting in the moonlight.
With its two alert ears nothing could pass by it
and its quick-minded brain would go for the kill.
A hunter who came was a man with a gun,
holding it up to aim.
But leopard did not want to become the great big human's game.
He sprung like a springbok as quick as a flash
and never was seen again.
In the silent black forest a rustle of the breeze is heard...
But this time it's the wind, whistling in the trees.

Anne McMillan

My Dog Isla

Here's my little friend,
With a wee brown nose and big loppy lugs,
A nice happy face,
My favourite dug.

She's happy and playful,
Rolling in the mud,
And her tail never stops wagging -
Thud, thud, thud!

She can play a good game of football,
Scores the ball in the goals,
And I never saw such a dog
For digging enormous holes!

Her nose can sniff so many smells.
Her eyes gleam like glass.
Her little feet run faster
Than any other bonnie lass.

She loves to play with wood and toys.
You couldn't call her meek
'Cause she always finds you quickly
In a game of Hide-and-seek.

She's kind and good and loving,
With her little ears that curl.
She's the most wonderful little dog
In the whole wide world!

Kirsten McMillan

Chinese Spare Ribs

The Snow Blizzard

One morning I woke and found
that a mass of snow was everywhere!
I went out and felt the biting cold air.
The snow fell down in endless showers,
a howling wind, a bitter cold air, the worst
of its kind -
what a blizzard!
- Enough the make the pine trees whine.
All electricity - off it goes;
the heating too, as well.
I'm so glad! But because the school is off,
no lessons learned.
So...off I go outside, and make
a snowman, white and thick,
a carrot nose, stones for buttons.
Everyone must envy it!
No Brownie Burns' Night.
No hot tea.
In all Dumfries and Galloway,
so much snow,
more than in 50 years,
the worst snow there's been in my life.
It's the worst in Britain - here.
We went sledging! One at a time
down the slopy hill. Tried to go
all at once, the whole three of us,
Graeme, Gary and I, but it didn't work.
No, no, no. Graeme fell over and hurt his head,
so did Gary, and so did I
- on top of the lot.
But we went home and had a drink -
mildly warm Ribena.
Daddy came in angry - a lot -
because of the snow, he couldn't work
as he had been doing.

Chinese Spare Ribs

The snow was lovely,
white and white, most beautiful white.
My little dog loves the snow.
She's really sad it's gone away.
And I wish, I really wish
the snow just wouldn't go.

Kirsten McMillan

Chinese Spare Ribs

The Bush

The bush is very little
and wants to be like dad,
but little bush is naughty
and nothing like his dad.
Soon the winter will be here
and baby will get cold, so he gets
covered over, and poor old dad
gets left in the cold.
When summer comes again,
dad is very old, baby is a dad
and dad is growing old.
Soon dad will die, and his son
will be all alone, lonely and so sad.
So his father had to go
but soon his father had to die.

Fiona McTaggart

The Coast

The cliffs
Guard the bay like sentries,
Tall and strong,
Gazing darkly at the manic gulls -
Vultures of the salty desert.

Circling with greedy anticipation,
They spy the fishing vessel far below -
The hunter proudly delivering its bounty to the shore,
Majestically ploughing the waves
That heedlessly carry on
Their relentless, rhythmical dance -
Gently sifting the sand,
As if searching
For lost time.

Lucy Mack

Spring

The fell wind and
Drich cauld dribbly weather's ower
For winter's gaen
And spring's beginning to kythe itsel

Bonnie flowers upward-springing
In gardens throughout the toon
Cantie and sonsie colourful and sweet
Brightening us up from our gloom

Wee lammies jinkin about the mailin
A chuckie wi her chicks
Mithers wi their calves snedin the grass
Watching the weans rantin and frisky

There's a cannie breeze and it's getting warmer
I might even go for a skiddle
Spring's here wi all its smeddum again
Bringing flowers new families and warm weather

Lois Marshall

My Brain

My brain is a bunch of curling tubes.
It is a squidgy piece of equipment
Which is stapled to my skull.
It feels like it is ready to explode
With its working too hard.
Wobbling like jelly when I move;
Pink and full of slime,
But simply rounded to a T.

Scott Maxwell

Chinese Spare Ribs

Pharaoh

Here I lie among the dead,

Jackal made and jackal fed.

When Osiris starts his reign

I will walk the world again.

Stewart Middleton

A Little Too Perfect

She lived in a frosted glass bubble,
Where flowers forever bloomed and the sun,
Dazzling, shone.
She was "Simply a pleasure to teach"; "An
Asset to the class".
She was the kind of pupil
Teachers would move
To influence others to the good.
She often wondered
How it would feel if the rain poured and
Her bubble became transparent.
She was expected to achieve
The highest grades;
"If she couldn't, who could?"
She felt trapped.
She scratched and clawed at her glass bubble
Until it shattered.
She watched splinters of sunshine
And grey lifeless flowers scatter.
She could imagine what they would say.
She felt an icy cold tear chill her cheek.
The bitter cold,
From which she had been shielded,
Stung her hands.
She knew.
This time she wouldn't smile sweetly
And explain in her angelic voice
To fit in with everyone's expectations.
She understood.
This finally was her chance to escape.
No one could understand why
For her life was so perfect.

Lisa Milne

Chinese Spare Ribs

The Glass Eye

My Gran had a glass eye
That peered at me as if it had a life of its own.
Devoid of feeling,
It was as cold as stone.
At night, she kept it in a glass of water,
And I, in fascination, would creep in to view it
As if the eye was an exhibit in a museum.
In the morning, the eye would be back in its daytime place,
Peering at me again.

Valla Moodie

Burns' Walk 19th January 1996

Rose hips flame red in the greyness.
Iron railings rise harsh and barren from amongst the winter
foliage.
Violets and primroses are just memories of summer.
Evergreens add a deep green to the brown of the dead river bank.
Rushing, swirling under-currents splash gently around the rocks.

Nests woven by summer birds lie tangled in the reeds.
Ice has melted and flowed downstream to the warm sea.
Trees are beginning to bud with signs of early spring.
Heat and warmth will soon arrive with a new summer
            and the banks will be alive once more.

Kirsty Muir

Summer Child

Someone appears in the doorway,
A Renoir,
A kaleidoscope of sunlit tones.
Her sleepy eyes, once opened -
Sapphires,
Dragonfly wings,
Tropical seas.
A cloud of spiders' silks envelopes her head -
Midday sun,
Prize nugget,
Wheat field.
Her hand pulls it away from her face -
English rose,
Coral reef,
Rare opal.
She smiles and the world turns.

Kirsty Muir

Chinese Spare Ribs

Symphony of War

The conductor takes the stage.
He coughs gently and opens his music.
He takes the thin baton in his hand and lifts it into the air;
The deep gentle roll of a drum breaks the silence.

The loud drone of aircraft engines fills the air,
People look up to the skies to see the familiar sight.
A dark foreboding shadow is cast over the city,
The high pitched siren starts wailing.

The violins pick up the melody,
Cellos and clarinets add volume and power to the music,
The drums become louder and louder until they are deafening.
The notes of the symphony echo through the stillness.
Cymbals crash.

The first bomb is dropped from overhead.
It explodes violently, showering the street with stones.
Women scream as they try to carry their children to safety.
More bombs fall, buildings collapse all around.
The flames spread quickly, creating a city of fire.
The noise of the aircraft, bombs and commotion is immense.

Huge tubas and horns blast out their deep notes,
The conductor's baton makes short, sharp gestures,
With every one a new instrument picks up a harmony.
One quick move and there is complete silence.
A drum wistfully beats out a slow march.

People slowly emerge from their hiding places.
Corpses lie strewn across the street
With the rubble and debris left by the enemy.
Families wander, looking for a familiar face
But find only death in their path.

Kirsty Muir

My Sister's Hair

My sister's hair
is brown.
It looks quite normal
but really
it's amazing!
One day
it jumped off her head
and danced about
the floor.
Another day
it put on some shades
a leather jacket
and bought itself
a handbag.
It jumped off her head
and went down to the
Junction.
My sister's hair
is sparkly clean
and she's always
colouring it
a different colour
every day.
The next day
she dyed it
red
which was very
silly
because she had
pink
mascara on.
When it got back to being brown
it decided to get a job
as a decorator.
But this was terrible

Chinese Spare Ribs

because you know how much
paint
you get in your hair
when painting.
But on Thursday
it went all out
and booked itself
for a bungee-jump.
It swung from the bridge
very elegantly
but the funniest thing
is
my sister never notices
anything
at all
ever.

Laura Muir

Your Invasion

This room is mine,
'Do NOT enter!'
Reads the sign,
Pinned to the door;
Yet you do.

I do not snoop
In your private affairs;
Yet you read my mail,
Take my stuff;
I don't get them back.

My room is my hideaway,
Yet you still invade.
You don't knock,
Just waltz in,
Like you belong here.

My room.
My stuff.
You don't belong here!
Get out!
STAY OUT!

Cheryl Muirhead

Birds Nest Anywhere

In stony quarries
or even old lorries

In a scarecrow's pocket
or an old power socket

In some old rusty kettles
or prickly nettles

Far out at sea
or in an old tree

On ploughed land
or in a tunnel in the sand

Down on the ground

Or high in the air

Everywhere!

Kyle Muirhead

She Hurts Ma Feelings

I dinnae want tae gan tae the Bingo the nicht
I would rether stay at hame and watch *Coronation Street*
That young woman she makes fun o me every nicht
And she hurts ma feelins
When she ta'ks aboot ma broun and ma grey hair
Me and her grandmither were gid friends at schule
but she just lauchs
I feel like pullin her glesses aff so she misses
a nummer!

Natasha Murdoch

My Love Is Like A Rainy Day

My Love is like a rainy day,
With dark clouds in the sky.
If I was seen around with him,
I would surely die.

My love is like a dark rain cloud,
His personality grey.
My love waits by the railway track
For trains to come his way.

For trains to come his way he waits,
Down by the railway track.
If I see him just one more time
Then I am going to crack.

He really is a little nerd,
But he is unawares
That people laugh out loud at him
As down the track he stares.

Claire Murray

To Stinking Socks

O stinking socks,
You make my shoes smell,
My feet, my bag, my room as well.
Your rotting, sweaty, cheesy hum
Gets me in trouble with my Mum.

O stinking socks,
You must be found!
Or else your smell will hang around.
You're in my room, lost in the mess.
Your hiding place I cannot guess.

O stinking socks,
Through stinking haze,
Upon your grotty heap I gaze.
I know you try not to be seen,
But soon enough, you will be seen.

O smelly socks,
I'm glad you're gone,
But I know it's not for long.
I have P.E. in three days' time,
And you'll be back and smelling fine.

Claire Murray

Frog

It sits calmly, waiting to swim,
Blowing up its huge throat.
Both of us savour
The sanguine mist.
Like a drawing
It is green and mundane.

It may be paranoia, but I think
It thinks that I'm thinking we're thinking
I have no prejudice against it,
But I never want it to blow up its mouth
Again,
Again.

Adam Nash

The Outcast

Dubbed when born,
An outlaw torn,
The thorn within
Society's kin,
No culture or race,
Just a sorry face,
No friends or voice,
No chance or choice,
You're left alone,
Sad and stranded,
The outcast is
What you've been branded.

Richard Nelson

My Special Friend

I have a very special friend,
As pretty as can be,
With golden hair and big blue eyes,
And freckles - just like me!

We share our taste in posters,
Her room is just like mine,
When I go out,
Well ... she does too.

She's happy when I give a smile,
And downcast when I frown.
If you're still guessing with deliberation,
I'm sorry, but ... it's only my reflection.

Denise Obern

You!

You! Your hair is like black snakes hanging.

You! Your breath stinks like rotten cheese.

You! Your beer-belly stomach hanging there.

You! Your narrow slit eyes staring that evil stare.

You! Your foamy mouth dripping like a dog with rabies.

You! Your fat beefy legs are like Cumberland sausages.

You! Your small snotty nose poking out of your face.

You! Your long pointy feet that get in the way.

You! Your ugly corgi dog that always fouls the pavements.

You! You're a disgrace to society.

You! Your day's a disappointment.

You! YOU'RE REVOLTING!

David Owen

Homework

Have you got a brother?
Yes Sir!
Have you got a mother?
Of course Sir!
What about your father?
Away Sir.
I'm sorry to hear that your father's not near
But - if you forget your homework
Three times this year
I'll take you to the office
Hand on ear!

Bret Park

Because It Was So Hot That Summer

Because it was so hot that summer
The snow drifts reached record heights
And the neighbouring tribe of mutant cucumbers went bananas.
They teamed up with the rebel gherkins
And collaborated to form the guerrilla group 'Veggi Warfare'
Which set about plundering all shops of peanut butter
And held the pink elephant for ransom,
Even though she protested her innocence
Of ever insulting a courgette about his welly boots.

Eventually the elephant eluded her captors
And abseiled up the wall to safety,
But, unfortunately,
Her tutu caught on the Boeing 747 stuck in the wall
And she plummeted down to the roof,
Where she promptly squidged a little old lady
Who happened to be practising the three-legged race
With her pet rhino named Cecil,
Who was the reigning world origami champion.

Luckily for Cecil, his expertly folded and flawlessly executed
Paper parachute enabled him to float without mishap
From under the feather weight bulk of the pink elephant,
Just in time to hear the announcement by his 'muscleness',
The Great Green Spinach,
That the day was to be a national holiday in celebration of the
Royal Society for the Prevention of Cruelty to Broccoli.

The mutant cucumbers and rebel gherkins were outraged by this,
But consoled themselves
By consuming vast quantities of peanut butter
And enrolling for origami lessons
Whilst reassuring the courgette
That his wellies were really very nice indeed.

Cara Paterson

Chinese Spare Ribs

Biolohoob

Absorption, Secretion, Contractile fibres -
Brain buzzing with biological bumf,
I entered the school,
Genotype, Phenotype, Monohybrid cross -
Nervous, nonsensical chatter stabs the electric atmosphere,
While forced smiles fail to reassure.
Chlorophyll, Xanthophyll, Mitochondrion -
"If we don't know it now, we never will,"
The words skim over my head.
Hypotonic, Isotonic, Cell epidermis -
Stay calm, stay cool, stay collected ... stay awake!
Maybe burning the midnight oil wasn't such a good idea.
Diphosphate, Triphosphate, Metabolic pathway -
Facts and figures spurt from my ears
And trickle from my nose.
Cytosine, Adenine, Deoxyribose sugar -
The doors open - this is it ...
No going back.
Monocyte, Lymphocyte, Phagocytosis -
Sitting at my desk with a bad case of the squeaks,
I organise my pens with military precision.
Diploid, Haploid, Recombinant DNA -
The paper is placed before me.
With a confident intake of breath, I glance down.
....***Lenin, Stalin, Russian Revolution -***
Uh oh.

Cara Paterson

Do You Take Drugs?

Drugs? Whit bugger **needs** them?

Ye'll hae mind o' the kinna thing:

"Ertifishil...stimulants, boys nd gels"

"Ehm sure we can be without, **ehrm,**

thet sort of thing, can we not**?**"

(Aye right, hen - you dae a' the takkin', jist let me **rest**)

"**Dirrti things** - they may well

give you, ahhm, some pleshir when you firrst

try them
but that soon wears off!?"

"addiction"; aye, jist, **adikshin**

soshal ostrichism - dearie me, the bliddy **shame** o' it

ah nearly forgot - depend'cy

like when you, hen, need to take two asprins; 'cause

one won't work any more ...

Christopher Phin

Chinese Spare Ribs

No More Elephants

I told people if they kept killing them they'd become extinct,
But did they listen ... No!

I told people if they kept shooting there would soon be none left,
But did they listen ... No!

I kept protesting against them doing it,
But did they listen ... No!

I told people if they killed them for their ivory and skin now
they couldn't kill them later,
But did they listen ... No!

I told people if they killed the mothers and fathers
then there wouldn't be any babies to kill,
But would they listen ... No!

I told people that if they let them die naturally
then they could still get their ivory and skin,
But did they listen ... No!

And are they happy now ... No!
They still want more.

Julie Pierce

Dragon

DRAGON

Great monster

Green scales glittering

Mythical creature breathing fire

Fierce

DRAGON

Ferocious hunter

Unfurling great wings

Fierce frightening fiery creature

Angry

Loreley Platt

Heroic

Heroic

blood-sucker

spins silk webs

cross patterned back

six silk producing spinnerets

eight legged hairy monster

discards old skins

blood thirsty

ARACHNID

Ross Preston

The Fat Door Mouse

Fat Fat Fat Fat
I know you're fat,
but you need to eat some more,
it's soon winter.
Try and eat the door
as you are a door mouse.
Eat the handle.
That would be nice.
Or the wood.
That would be nice too.
I do not like wood or handles either.
I thought you were a door mouse, boy.

Alan Provost

Eyemouth Bay

One day outside old Eyemouth Bay
There was a very bad storm and the sky was grey.
Before this day is done I say
Wives and mothers will cry this day
In old Eyemouth Bay.

A tanker with oil was in dire straits.
Two ships with fish were coming too close.
A bang and a crash and they all went down.
Mothers will cry this day
In old Eyemouth Bay.

Three-hundred died that day
Outside old Eyemouth Bay.
One lady who was walking her dog on the bay
Saw a flash and bang,
So she ran to say
There had been a disaster
In old Eyemouth Bay.

Rescuers say it was hard to get there that day
As the waves went crashing in old Eyemouth Bay,
But they fought and toiled all night until day break.
Then you see the real heartbreak
Of the horror in Eyemouth Bay.

Alan Rae

Flower Arranging

The roses,
I place them carefully,
Treasuring their fragility now they are
Dried, like the tears
I never shed.
Could I have
Let them flow

Like thoughts?
I'm finding it easier,
Arranging; remembering is
Harder, more painful. But now
The roses, reminders
Of happiness
Past and present.

Bliss continuing
An everyday miracle -
Tidying - my jumbled box
Slowly filling with items
To be filed
Under unpresent
And pleasant:

The love
I never felt before,
Encouraging me to destroy
Flowerless pasts.
For the future
Shows it was never
Worth hoarding.

Hannah Reeve

Chinese Spare Ribs

The Mushroom Ballad

"Well ye shouldna tak' acid," the polisman said,
"Or ye'll ruin yer life, an' ye'll end up dead."

Sae ah didnae tak' acid, but mushrooms instead,
An' ah still nearly died an' ended up dead.

Fur the world went mad an' swirled a' aroon,
As a big green alien knocked me richt doon.

Ma knees were a' scraped an' ma bluid wus blae
An' ah said tae ma mates, "I luv ye, ah dae!"

"Ye're oot o' yer heid," ma mates cried oot.
"Ah'm ah nuthin'. Let's gaan up the wood!"

"Whit the hell wis that?" "It's only an owl."
"Ah dinnae hink sae, it sounds like a howl."

"It's a friggin' wolf!" "Aye, right. Get away!"
"It is ah tell ye, an it's comin' this way!"

Well they a' scarpered aff an' on tae the street,
But cus ah wus trippin' ah fell ower ma feet.

They left me ahin', a' on ma ain,
When ah froze wi terror as the wolf howled again.

But it wusnae a wolf : it wus the polis.
Ah wus that bloody scared that ah needed a piss.

Well ah legged it real fast, but ah fell on ma face,
Sae the polis - they caught me. "You're comin' back tae base."

This filled me wi' terror. Ma heid cleared richt quick
As they carted me aff, richt doon tae the nick.

Noo ah've learnt ma lesson, an' ah've learnt it well.
Ye dinnae tak' mushrooms - fur ye get intae hell.

Hannah Reeve

Chinese Spare Ribs

The Wizard Idea

Gone.
Moved away.
Left behind, the empty house,
a damp, empty shell.
Full of mice - and memories.

You didn't want to go,
but you had no choice.
Another of your stepdad's wizard ideas.
'Return to his childhood' - so he said.
New house. New life.
New friends.
Better friends, possibly.

A letter.
Newsy, funny.
Homesick.
'The football's better.
They call me "Boncan" here.
What's life like back there?'

'Back there.'
Home.
Your real home, where I sit
and read your letters.
Waiting for the next one.
Waiting for you to return.
There was no reason to leave;
you shouldn't have left.
Life was fine here,
but you moved anyway.
Some wizard idea.

Hannah Reeve

Chinese Spare Ribs

The Door

The door opens and closes
A crack of light appears regularly
Lighting up my dark room
A strip of yellow colours my room.

The door opens and closes
With an eerie creak
The hinges squeak in rhythm
As the door caresses the wooden floor.

The door opens and closes
Outside there is snow on the ground
A blanket of white over my garden
A cat's footprints break into the smoothness

The door opens and closes.

Lindsay Reid

Winter Haiku

Snow in the garden
A cat's paws
Break the whiteness.

Lindsay Reid

Somebody

Somebody's out there, I know there is,
But the problem is, I don't know who.
It's somebody mean.
It's somebody wicked.
There's got to be, I know there is.
If there's not, then
Why are all those children missing?
This is a tricky one.
I wonder
Who.
I wonder
Why.
I don't know who,
What, why or how.
Who would do such a thing?
Somebody menacing,
Round the town.
Why does it have to be so hard?
Why does it
Have to be so tricky?
When I look around the town,
All I can see is a mess.
If there really is somebody out there,
All I want to know is who!

Charlotte Richardson

Dad'th Mouth

Brown,
Furry,
Thmall.

Hazel Rigg

The Town By Night

The silence is broken.
A car speeds past
Till it shrinks to a speck
In the distance.
Silence, again!

A mother stumbles past,
Two children behind,
Being dragged on their heels,
Kicking and screaming.
Silence, again!

Two men wandering aimlessly,
Their wives frantically trying to control them.
They start to sing in a slurred voice.
You can see where they've been.
Silence, again!

A late night jogger next,
His reflective clothing glints in the street lights.
The sound of trainers pattering the pavement,
Till he turns the corner into darkness.
Silence, again!

The street is lifeless.
The shadows are the only sign of movement.
Lights flicking on, then off.
People going to bed.
Silence, again.

Stuart Roan

Duick

I'm no as graceful as the eagle,
Swoopin' o'er the scree.
I'm jist a plain an ornar duick,
An that's aw I want tae be.

I'm no as colourful as the puffin,
Livin' next tae the sea.
I'm jist a plain an ornar duick,
An that's aw I want tae be.

I'm no a gymnast like the blue tit,
Hangin' frae a tree.
I'm jist a plain an ornar duick,
An that's aw I want tae be.

I'm quite, quite different frae the others,
Who aren't a bit like me.
I'm jist a plain an ornar duick,
An that's aw I want tae be.

Rebecca Ross

Swan

See her gentie in the air,
This bonnie bird in flicht,
Lang craigit an' wi' wings oot-stretched -
A swan - an amazin' sicht.

Frae an oosie broon tuft o' doon
The cygnet growes sae fast,
Every day mair elegant-like
Till a beautiful swan at last.

Rebecca Ross

Chinese Spare Ribs

Waiting

"10.15".
Still waiting.
Radio Two. Something blasts out.
Terry Wogan.
Sweaty hands slip on orange plastic chairs.
Find myself reading *Farmers Journals*.
Everyone stares.
Nobody looks.
Old women sit near.
Smell like broth.
They sit and shake pill bottles.
"10.45".
Fat woman and man.
Come out a white room holding a bag of inhalers.
Still waiting.
Turn my head.
Slowly.
Man stares again.
Like a monkey after a biscuit.
Turn away.
"11.00".
Called up.
Walk slowly.
Open the swing door.
Bang! Hits you fast.
Big doctor smile.
Class A.
Unwillingly grin back.
Snaps white rubber gloves.
Look at calm white walls.
Spongy cream carpet.

Jerome Scherrer

Chinese Spare Ribs

Old Car

An old car is a dead beetle.
Lying on the ground
Rotting like an old pile of leaves
It looks like two rectangles
With their corners cut off
And sat on top of each other.
The car has no sound,
Just like a book on a shelf.
It smells like burnt rubber
And is rough like a cheese grater.
When I look at it I think about
How it could have been mine.

Craig Scott

The Big Parade

Weighed down with boots
And an oversized jacket,
I struggled desperately,
Trying to climb onto the lorry.

A helping hand
Came from above,
Hauling me up.

Jolting steadily forward,
As the silvery drops
Fell from the sky.

The sky cleared.
The golden face showed itself.

Waving and shouting at strangers,
Strangers waving back.

All of us forgetting our cause
In the excitement,
Balloons bouncing
Like buoys on a rough sea.

Turning a corner,
Thrust forward
Into a jungle of people we go,
Joined together,
Yet far apart.

Colours light up
And dance
In front of our eyes.

Chinese Spare Ribs

Crowds dispersing,
Somebody still waving
Screams fading
Into time.

Journey ending,
Tired, no voice, but happy.
Friends joining silently.
Guid Nychburris is over.

Rowena Alexa Seagrave

Hibernating

May the cold winter breeze blow
and come down the snow.
Curl up.
Let the rain pour
and the thunder roar.
In a ball you are.
Spring's so far.
Coldness is here.
Wrap up tight.

Come out - it is spring,
hear the birds sing -
out of your hole.
Winter's gone.
Spring's won.

Sapphire Skillen

My Old Farm

I once lived on a farm on a hill-top so high,
Where the clouds met the mountains as the seasons passed by,
Where the bright summer sun blessed our few acres of land.
   'A new life of prosperity' is what we had planned.

The springtime meant lambing, a source of great joy,
Remembering the times when I stood as a boy,
Watching them lie on their fleece cotton white,
   Their eyes tightly closed as they shut out the light.

The month of July saw no rain, not a drop,
The fields were ablaze with corn, our new crop.
Large harvesters roared as their blades slashed and spun,
   Our work was completed as it had always been done.

The warm autumn colours of trees by the byre.
I remember the gales as I huddled by the fire.
When the last bale of straw had been used from the load,
   A murderous 'For Sale' sign appeared at the end of our road.

One last turn of the key and it was time for the off.
I couldn't think of my farm being owned by a toff,
This place I had loved and had wanted to stay,
   But a new farm was beckoning. It was time to move away.

Nigel Smallwood

Which Witch Watched!

Which witch watched me
down in the quay
Which witch did I watch
was it Hilda or was it Cyclops
Which witch stole my watch
down in the corner shop
Which witch did I miss
when she blew me a hideous kiss

WHICH WITCH WATCHED!

Lewis Smith

The Cool Blue

Blue is the colour of the sea.
Blue is the colour of the water.
Blue is like a cool rap.

Get down with blue.
Get down with blue.
Get down with blue.

Blue is like an icepack.
Blue is like the sky.
Blue is like a tear.

Sam Smith

All Of Me

Truth or lie - live or die -
Be or not - free or caught -
Ask or tell - hiss or yell -
Whole or half - cry or laugh -
Make or break; for goodness' sake
Can't you see? It has to be.

Hide or seek - bold or meek -
Forward or shy, defer, comply -
Do or dream - smile or scream -
Hot or cold - asked or told.
Be a man (you know you can)
Be girl and grasp the world.

Have it all - or not at all.
Life's too short. Hold that thought.

Emily Stevens

Mirror Image

I lift my right hand,
she lifts her left.
The room there, on the other side
is the wrong way round.
It strikes me, she would
have had to learn to read
backwards ...
If I smile, she smiles.
She shares my pain - or
do I share hers?
But I wink and she
doesn't wink back - I scream
and she laughs
... from the other side.

Emily Stevens

Chinese Spare Ribs

Five Quiet Haiku

Midnight tears run
down your face and dry there
as the sun rises

Eyes shine through darkness
as clouds drift across the moon
the cat stalks the night

Our conversation
became so deep we surfaced
on the other side

Snowflakes drift to Earth
and conceal the countryside
a little white lie

A house on the water
floats down the river watching
the tow paths go by

Emily Stevens

Sounds

I love the sound of a
crystal cave with icicles
tingling the frosted air.
I love the sound of a
snowflake falling and
hitting the hard packed snow,
the sound of an eye blinking,
the sound of a
shell calling the sea,
a beast calling the wild
on a moonlit night
in the middle of winter.

I hate the sound of a
long cold scream
sending shivers up your back,
the sound of an old
rusty voice
breaking cold stiff silences
going through your head
like a blacksmith hammering
or a hunter shooting
and a life falling
into a stone cold tomb.

Tracy Thom

Chinese Spare Ribs

The Dead House

based on a theme from a novel by Kathleen Fidler

As the man
Held the torch,
He set the thatch alight.
Whoosh!
Red blood flames
Gushed out of the roof
Like a bleeding wound.
Yellow flames sharply spewed
Out of the door devouring
Anything in their path.
Thick black smoke bellowed
Out of the roof, choking
The house to death.
Screaming!
Howling!
Screeching!
And all that remains is
The Dead House...

Aaron Thomson

I'd Rather Be

I'd rather be warm than cold
   I'd rather be left than told

I'd rather be young than old
   I'd rather be dull than bold

I'd rather be bought than sold
   I'd rather be pushed than pulled

I'd rather be free than called
   I'd rather be flat than rolled

I'd rather be fooled
   I'd rather be empty than full

Kay Thorburn

Myra Ratter

Myra Ratter is old and withered.
Her hair is like a clump of burned moor heather.
Her coat is long and dusty grey.
Her eyes have almost shrunk away.

She looks at you with gloom and then
Her tiny eyes glint and fade again.
Perhaps she's a witch come from the past.
Perhaps her life is fading fast.
Perhaps no one will ever know
Quite who she is or where she goes.
She never speaks, but walks alone.
She travels, never has a home.
When she visits our town
People scorn her with wary frowns.
They shun her, hate her, walk away,
So she moves on more with every day.
Her steps are light, despite her age.
She really looks a wise old sage.
Her smile is like a wisp of smoke.
Her neck's so thin that she might choke.
Her back is most uncommonly straight.
She seems to me of no great weight.
Like a shadow, she glides round corners dark
And disappears without a mark.
Mysterious, I know that's true:
So, Myra Ratter, who are you?

Louise Trowbridge

The Sinking Of The Titanic

The Titanic sat in the harbour
As thousands piled onto her deck.
Nobody thought, in a few days' time
All she would be was a wreck.

One night when everyone was dancing,
The Titanic ran out of her luck.
The captain thought nothing could sink his ship,
But he was wrong 'cause an iceberg struck.

Nobody seemed to worry;
Nobody seemed to care.
The Titanic was slowly sinking
Because of the huge big tear.

The captain got very worried,
And began to fix the lifeboats.
None of the passengers noticed,
Until the women and children got floats.

People began to notice it was serious.
They began to push and fight.
Someone lit up a flare for help
And there was a sudden burst of light.

Their calls for help were useless,
Nobody seemed to hear.
The band kept on playing,
But it didn't get rid of the fear.

The lifeboats were lowered,
Leaving the men on the ship.
All you could hear were the screams for help,
As the Titanic began to tip.

She slowly sank into the sea,
Like a coffin being lowered into the ground.
The Titanic plummeted into the depths of the ocean,
Never ever to be found.

Ashley Walker

Chinese Spare Ribs

Lonely Cheap Glove

You sit there unknowingly pointing at me,
a line of fluff outlines your point.

You sit there but no one likes you,
not a mother could love you -
you're man made.

Lost in a country far away from Taiwan,
a cheap pattern covering
your empty inside.

You've not got a maker's tag,
no one's proud of you.
You've not got a name tag,
happy to lose you.

You're alone and useless,
no pocket will hide you.
You sit scared and unhappy - divorced.

Sarah Watson

Megrin

Ye bully ma braine.
Ye chew ma temple.
Ye snigger an play yer bairn games.

Ye rin tae ma ear
an then tae ma een.
Oh heidaiche, rin awa fae me!

Sarah Watson

Precious Bairn

The bairn hides,
balancing on our world.
The bairn hides,
his protective boat rocks like a cradle.

Escape our dark world
before missiles strike you.
Escape this dark world
while you've still water to sail in.

Keep your head low
as the tankers swagger past you.
Protect your wee head
as you hear submarines below.

Sail away from the wars
and hatred, out of control.
Sail away where you're safe.
Find a new home.

Sarah Watson

Address Tae A Cra'

There ye sit,
Yin, twa or mair.
It isny fair for ither birds -
like houlets for yin.
They're oot at nicht,
they hud their wheesht,
those silent wings,
except for the odd keech.
There's micht in 'em.
So next time you see a cra'
think o' the houlet.

Angus Wemyss

Peregrine

The graceful Peregrine swoops for prey down
through the guiding air.
A jet-like predator,
with eyes that are deadly and fatal.
The falcon's talons,
blood-gripped, skin-ripping,
could be fatal even at sight.
The bill of death,
wire-skinning, meat-mauling,
is specialised for even a mighty victim.
As this mechanical hunting predator gets ready for
the danger flight,
the surroundings will seal it.
Now the death moment has come.
It has its speed wings.
It has its blood talons.
It has its meat bill.
It has its death eyes.

Angus Wemyss

Swan

A feather-bed floats across a
still lake.
The fur-lined radiator - perfect for a game of
hide and go seek - is a QE2, a floating
hotel.
As the young cygnet tourists
wait for the white liner to return
from its "Tour around the Lake",
they themselves
may have a tour of their own.

Angus Wemyss

The White Harbour (Port Ban)

No one knows where the magic starts.
How? Why?
The secret only lies beneath the machair
and there it will lie.
What is it? Don't ask me, but it lies beneath the sea,
and only this land is sand.

You pictured a fishing village, I hear,
combining the sea and the sand?
You don't understand.
You can't see our land.

Ban is white.
A *Port* is a harbour.

Now you have entered
our land.

Angus Wemyss

Chinese Spare Ribs

Love

Love is a
log floating down
a stream.
One minute you
see it,
the next minute
it has gone.

Love is a rose
you can't sniff.
You know you want
to marry her,
but you can't.

Patrick Wemyss

Sounds I Like

Cows breathing heavily
like monsters chasing you
through a forest at night time.

The sound of barnacles
pulling themselves to the rocks
like cereal
when you pour milk onto it.

I hate the sound of hail against
a window when you have
a headache, or
an unoiled wheel
going round and round.

Patrick Wemyss

The Tree People

The tree people
the tree people
don't disturb the
tree people

or else ...
they'll boil your toes
eat your nose
use your tongue as
a cover for their bed
that's what they
said.

So don't disturb the
tree people.

The tree people
are green
most are in
their teens
they'll bash you
if you go
near them.
SO DON'T DISTURB
THE TREE
PEOPLE!

Patrick Wemyss

Chinese Spare Ribs

Beat The Devil

The black eagle rises, the earth it scolds,
While its people worship their lord of gold.
He's not my god, God knows he's not yours.
The eagle, laughing while blood seeps from its pores.

You can't beat the devil, so join at his side.
Hold aloft the crooked cross, salute him as he rides.
Never try to argue, accept it as your fate.
You're only one of millions who by his side will wait.

A young man wears a brown shirt. Proud, loyal, bold.
He holds his head up high as they welcome him to their fold.
Shylock was a rich man. Shylock had to die.
If at first the solution's not clear to see, then open up your eyes.

Some say he is a good man, others don't agree.
Left with a distant feeling that once they were more free.
The only problem with life is death, and soon it came his way,
But the millions he took with him are remembered still today.

His shadow swallowed nations, his regime based on fear.
His character was ruthless, his policies were clear.
Don't let him take his pound of flesh, just cut him down to size,
And now the devil has returned, stand firm, oppose his rise.

Neil C. Westgarth

Revolution

Blood stained the tarmac battlefield,
The air began to clear,
In a city whose streets are littered with bodies,
And whose people live in fear.
Hell's fire burns, reveals the dead of night,
And "mercy" is a forgotten word.
Inside, the atrocities are clear as day;
outside, they remain unheard.

Yet they say "Join the revolution!"
They say they'll set your country free,
And, though I daren't say it'll turn out that way,
We'll just have to wait and see.

One more day, and one more life
Is taken from the sniper's nest.
Burning houses light the streets at night,
And streetlamps light the rest.
A coffin is carried through the streets of the city,
Its colours are green and white.
Living by the rule that right is wrong,
And two wrongs make a right.

They say that it's a Holy War.
But surely God can't approve.
Although the glory's gone, still their swords are drawn.
Secret armies are on the move.

The city still stands, but nothing is done
To enhance its people's lives.
And the government say they're taking steps
To blunt the terrorists' knives.
But a young man lies dead, gunned down in cold blood,
And who the hell gives a damn?

Chinese Spare Ribs

Just one more headstone over one more grave,
And one more death on some dirty hands.

Yet they say "Join the revolution!"
They say they'll set your country free,
And, though I daren't say it'll turn out that way,
We'll just have to wait and see.

They say that it's a Holy War.
But surely God can't approve.
Although the glory's gone, still their swords are drawn.
Secret armies are on the move.

Neil C. Westgarth

Savages

We moved across their homelands
Like the early morning light.
They'd called it their own for centuries
But now they had no rights.
We seized control of the hunting grounds,
Left carcasses to rot.
The beasts they killed to live on,
For sport our hunters shot.

They took their scalps in self-defence,
We took our scalps for kicks.
Then we held them up as devils
For copying our tricks.
The greatest hunters known to man
Before we gave them guns.
No more skill or fighting stealth
To pass down to their sons.

Still, they were merely savages
With paganistic ways,
So we burned their homes then we buried their bones
And gave them the rights of slaves.
Their lands now support a nation,
From their lands our people feed.
Their culture, still a mystery,
Wiped out by the white man's greed.

Neil C. Westgarth

Chinese Spare Ribs

Reindeer Thief

Reins are made of pricey leather
Ears are pointing to the ceiling
In my bedroom
No one knows I stole it except Debbie
Debbie says I am a prat
Eats my plants and revision papers
Everyone is getting suspicious
Reindeer are definitely not house pets.

The grotto's back door was open so I pushed him in
He caught me and threatened to call the police
I just did it for a laugh, I told him
Everyone was staring at my red face
From Santa and his Elves I ran home.

Stacy Williams

The Attic

As I looked into the gloom I saw:
An old carpet in patterns like swirling nebulae;
A baseball card;
A mummified cat;
A stuffed crocodile with burning green eyes.

As I looked deeper in the gloom I saw:
A bullet with the initials Z.A.;
An old pair of glasses with a spiral crack;
An old tape, green with age;
A camera with an undeveloped film;
A director's chair with a bullet hole.

As I looked at the back of the gloom I saw
A family trapped inside a painting but alive to the end.

Ian Wright

Sea

Black murky shadows creeping up the spiral curving pillars.
Waves crashing up above while soft breezes like currents
Twist into darkness.
Dark mysterious mystical fish curve in a world of never ending
madness.
The sunken city supplies safety from swirling never ending blackness.
Swirling coral cling tight to the grey hard rocks
For the gulping insanity would suck its lifeless body off the rocks.
Dark shapes start to emerge from the sandless bottom of the sea.
Life no longer in the underwater world
That was never found.

Ian Wright

Chinese Spare Ribs

Hippo And Lion

Hippo, said lion,
why do you go to the lake of Maho
where fishes swim and bing-bongs grow,
where crocodiles roam for possums so slow
and snakes like bedpans fly with the crows?

Lion, said hippo,
what do you know
of the land where bing-bongs grow,
where birds can't fly and bananas run wild
and cheetahs are slow and chickens run free in the snow,
and at twelve o'clock on every noon
the budgie sings songs to the moon,
and on every night of every day
May gets mixed up with June?

But why do you go to the lake of Maho,
where fishes swim and bing-bongs grow,
where apples are blue and cows can't moo
and chickens run free in the snow?

Lion, said hippo,
you never will know
of the land where the bing-bongs grow,
where bananas run wild and cheetahs are slow
and chickens play free in the snow.

Ian Wright

Flower Murder

As I walk through the lifeless garden I look around at all the flowers.
The moon shines on the fresh light crispy dew.
But one unwanted plant sits there waiting for me.
Its swarming evil body stands out like firs.
It bears no flowers, just evil sliding leaves.
It does not reflect magic moonlight but the dark blackness of the Devil.
It sits among the helpless young flowers,
Choking them as if it wanted something but couldn't
Because it wants only evil
And there is nothing evil about the young flowers.
A cold breeze runs down my back.
It starts to turn into masses of unstoppable madness.
It has very few foes.
Its horrible heavy snake-like figure bores through every nook and cranny.
I just wish it would curl up and die.
As it devours the flowers I feel a hot sticky tear run down my face.
My anger piles up in a heap.
Suddenly it bursts out like a balloon.
I rip it out by the neck and pull off its greedy head.
There is green blood shed as I crunch it in my hand.
Suddenly the hour-glass runs out.
I know my time is up.
So I decide to go back to my moonlit house.

Ian Wright

Chinese Spare Ribs

The Intruder

In the darkness of the night, when all is still,
A nasty piece of work sets out for the kill.
It travels so fast, but in total silence,
And it doesn't use fire or any violence.
Its aims are the defenceless and the weak.
It'll pick on an onion; possibly a leak.
When it's finished and time to move on,
In an instant it'll be gone.
But it leaves behind a distinctive trail.
A crisp coating covers everything, from head to tail,
A coating so bright, a coating so icy,
Like thousands of diamonds - just not so pricey,
Like broken glass shattered from above.
It shows no sign of caring, no sign of love.
When the moon's gone to bed - sun's rising high
Like a bright yellow button sewn to the sky
- Slowly the frost will retreat, disappearing in the air,
But it will be back tonight. - Try to stop it
If you dare.

Shonagh Wright

AGE CATEGORY AND YEAR OF ENTRY OF POEMS

1. UNDER 10:

Birds Nest Anywhere, Kyle Muirhead, 1998
The Chalk Board, Thomas Dagnon, 1995
Chinese Spare Ribs, Sam Allison, 1994
The Cool Blue, Sam Smith, 1997
The Dead Eagle, Derek Crook, 1998
Dragon, Loreley Platt, 1994
Duick, Rebecca Ross, 1997
Florida, Darryn Glen, 1998
Flower Murder, Ian Wright, 1995
Fairground Blues, James Henderson, 1995
The Fat Door Mouse, Alan Provost, 1994
A Friend Is..., Mark Henderson, 1994
Hello, Slimy, Slithery Snail, Tessa Bartlett, 1994
Heroic, Ross Preston, 1994
Hibernating, Sapphire Skillen, 1994
Hurcheon, George Clark, 1998
Jason, Chris Litherland, 1997
The Leopard, Anne McMillan, 1996
Love, Patrick Wemyss, 1996
My Dog Isla, Kirsten McMillan, 1996
My Mother, Gemma Bryant, 1998
Number Castle, Darren Maclean, 1998
Outside, Molly Bruce, 1996
Penguins, Emma Baillie, 1995
Peregrine, Angus Wemyss, 1995
The Puddock, Joanna Lane, 1998
Sea, Karin Jamieson, 1997
Sea, Ian Wright, 1995
Shadow, Chris Litherland, 1997
The Snow Blizzard, Kirsten McMillan, 1996
Somebody, Charlotte Richardson, 1997
Sounds I Like, Patrick Wemyss, 1996
The Strange Bag, Kirsty McIntyre, 1997
Swan, Rebecca Ross, 1997
Swan, Angus Wemyss, 1995
To Stinking Socks, Claire Murray, 1998

Chinese Spare Ribs

Tod, Rosie Georgeson, 1998
Trainspotting, Claire Finlay, 1998
The Tree People, Patrick Wemyss, 1996
Water Is For..., Liam Harkness, 1994
Wetland, Lorna Howe, 1995

2. UNDER 14:

A Little Too Perfect, Lisa Milne, 1998
Address Tae A Cra', Angus Wemyss, 1996
The Attic, Ian Wright, 1996
Back-Biting, Mark E. McLeod, 1995
Beachcomber, Wilma Garrett, 1995
Bullying, Sari Easton, 1995
The Bush, Fiona McTaggart, 1996
The Burning of Culmalie, Michael Diggins, 1995
Casualty, Jamie Burgess, 1995
The Coast, Lucy Mack, 1998
Computerollergy, Shontishar Hyslop, 1997
Dad'th Mouth, Hazel Rigg, 1998
The Dead House, Aaron Thomson, 1995
The Dentist From Hell, Emma McIntyre, 1998
Doctor's Waiting Room, Mary Carson, 1994
The Dolphin, Catriona Fitzsimon, 1997
The Door, Lindsay Reid, 1994
Explosive Anger, Lorna Hamilton, 1995
Eyemouth Bay, Alan Rae, 1994
Father To A Child, Aimee Cook, 1997
Friday 13th of November, Rodney Kane, 1994
Frog, Adam Nash, 1995
The Glass Eye, Valla Moodie, 1995
Hippo And Lion, Ian Wright, 1997
Homework, Bret Park, 1996
I'd Rather Be!, Kay Thorburn, 1998
The Intruder, Shonagh Wright, 1994
The Lake, Lorna Hamilton, 1995
My Brain, Scott Maxwell, 1995
My Ex-Best Friend, Katie Ferguson, 1997
My Love Is Like A Rainy Day, Claire Murray, 1997
My Sister's Hair, Laura Muir, 1997
My Special Friend, Denise Obern, 1995
Myra Ratter, Louise Trowbridge, 1995

Chinese Spare Ribs

No More Elephants, Julie Pierce, 1995
Old Car, Craig Scott, 1997
The Old Woman, Chris Litherland, 1998
A Pacifist In Wartime, Tali Burgess, 1998
The Plant, Allison Garrett, 1995
Pharaoh, Stewart Middleton, 1996
The Price, Kirstin Howatson, 1995
Reindeer Thief, Stacy Williams, 1998
Remembrance Day 11.11.18, Marie Cartner, 1994
Rush Hour, Kirsty Carswell, 1994
Scuil, Emma Baillie, 1996
The Sea, Lorna McIntyre, 1996
She Hurts Ma Feelings, Natasha Murdoch, 1996
The Sinking of the Titanic, Ashley Walker, 1994
Sounds, Tracy Thom, 1996
Spring, Lois Marshall, 1995
Stalked, Louise Johnstone, 1994
A Tom Boy, Emma Baillie, 1997
The Town By Night, Stuart Roan, 1994
Which Witch Watched!, Lewis Smith, 1996
The White Harbour (Port Ban), Angus Wemyss, 1996
Wind, Adam Crossan, 1995
Winter Haiku, Lindsay Reid, 1994
You!, David Owen, 1995
Your Invasion, Cheryl Muirhead, 1994

3. UNDER 18:

Afraid of the Dark, Allison McFarlane, 1998
All Of Me, Emily Stevens, 1997
The American Dream From Hope, Audrey Blair, 1994
Angel Of The Sun, Jodi Fraser, 1997
Beat the Devil, Neil C. Westgarth, 1994
Because It Was So Hot That Summer, Cara Paterson, 1996
The Big Parade, Rowena Alexa Seagrave, 1994
Bioloboob, Cara Paterson, 1997
The Bunnet-Laird, Annie Copland, 1995
Burns' Walk 19th January 1996, Kirsty Muir, 1996
Childhood, Nicola Gordon, 1997
Death As A Stranger, Lorna McAuley, 1996
Do You Take Drugs?, Christopher Phin, 1998
Five Quiet Haiku, Emily Stevens, 1998

Chinese Spare Ribs

Flower Arranging, Hannah Reeve, 1996
Fragments of Memories, Tasha Crofton, 1997
Harvest Moon, Matthew Chanarin, 1998
The Innocent Face, David Govier, 1994
Just Sitting : In Scotland, Holly Clay, 1994
The Lockerbie Air Disaster - 21st December 1988, Alanna Barron, 1994
Lonely Cheap Glove, Sarah Watson, 1995
Megrin, Sarah Watson, 1995
Michael, Holly Clay, 1996
Mirror Image, Emily Stevens, 1998
Morning, Laura Jackson, 1997
The Mushroom Ballad, Hannah Reeve, 1995
My Old Farm, Nigel Smallwood, 1994
The Outcast, Richard Nelson, 1998
Precious Bairn, Sarah Watson, 1995
Reflection, Kevin Lennon, 1995
Revolution, Neil C. Westgarth, 1994
Rock Woman, Stevie Docherty, 1997
Rubbish Dump, Elkie Hamid, 1994
The Sailor, Lorna McAuley, 1996
Savages, Neil C. Westgarth, 1994
Scarecrow, Annie MacFarlane, 1996
Song of the Battery Hen, Alanna Barron, 1994
Storm, Selena Dickson, 1996
Summer Child, Kirsty Muir, 1997
Symphony of War, Kirsty Muir, 1996
3 a.m., Kelly Clapperton, 1998
Two-Score Walkers In The Woods, David Govier, 1997
Waiting, Jerome Scherrer, 1997
The Wizard Idea, Hannah Reeve, 1994
The Worries of a Sinner, Lisa McLean, 1998

Chinese Spare Ribs

Chinese Spare Ribs

Chinese Spare Ribs

Chinese Spare Ribs